Chasing Zeroes

Chasing Zeroes

THE RISE *of* STUDENT DEBT,
the FALL *of the* COLLEGE IDEAL,
and ONE OVERACHIEVER'S
MISGUIDED PURSUIT *of* SUCCESS

By Laura Newland

STONE HALL PRESS

Design by Dennis Gallagher/visdesign.com
Editing by Elissa Rabellino/BaysideBookworks.com
Proofreading by Mark Rhynsburger
Author photograph by Sarah Jenkins

Stone Hall Press
PO Box 10050
Chicago, IL 60610
First printing, 2013

Printed in the United States of America

ISBN 978-0-9897765-0-9

For Mom and Dad

Contents

AUTHOR'S NOTE

It was only at the very end of college, as I reflected on four years that had unfolded in a way I never anticipated, that I had the idea to share my experience. As I wrote, I relied primarily on my own recollections and supplemented these by revisiting e-mails, talking to many of those involved, and researching relevant events that had occurred at the time. To condense an entire college experience into what I hope is a concise narrative, I occasionally reordered, modified, or combined events, conversations, and characters in minor ways that do not affect the substance of my story. I changed the names and identifying details of most, but not all, characters to protect the privacy of individuals. The names of companies are accurate, except in a few instances where I note the use of a pseudonym.

Prologue

EVERYONE LIES ON the first question. The interviewer expects it, and the interviewee accepts that honesty does not buy membership in one of this country's most exclusive clubs. The question and its deceptive answer are not a ritual or a joke, but a signal. To lie is to prove you understand the unwritten rules of a game that is governed by the irrational; to lie *well* is to prove you belong on Wall Street.

On a cold January afternoon during my junior year at Duke University, I prepared to deliver my own version of the lie for the most intimidating and influential judge I had ever faced—a Goldman Sachs banker and final-round interviewer for the preeminent bank's summer internship program. After welcoming me into his office and pointing out the stunning view of Manhattan that shone through his 40th-floor window, the financier—an attractive and sharply dressed man named Aidan—took a seat, folded his arms, and addressed me.

"So, Laura," he said with a cheeky grin. He leaned back in his chair and, as he stared out the window, asked the seemingly simple two-word question, "Why finance?"

I immediately breathed a slight, and hopefully unnoticeable, sigh of relief. I was grateful that Aidan chose to follow tradition by kicking off my interview with the standard opening. It was an invitation to deliver my polished answer, a response I had assembled months earlier but continued to refine until it met Goldman Sachs's impossibly strict standards. In its finished form, the brief speech struck the perfect balance of confidence, charm, and authenticity. To Aidan it would sound as if choosing a finance career came naturally to me, when in fact there was nothing natural about it at all.

This simple and straightforward question—*Why finance?*—sounds easy. And for the college students doggedly pursuing this career path, it *should* be. Yet, when I began preparing my response, I reacted just as many of my peers did. I panicked. Explaining why I wanted to be a banker seemed far more daunting than facing any of the other highly probable scenarios that make Wall Street interviews infamous: convoluted brainteasers, unpredictable financial trivia, and bullying at the hands of your interviewer. First, I had struggled to learn the complex rules that accompany such a basic question. Then, I had struggled to follow them. As a 20-year-old who had never taken a finance course, I found it difficult to explain why I found banking interesting without mentioning money, status, or the fact that I simply did not know what else to do with my life. It would be not only shameful but disastrous to admit that after watching so many peers cash in their diplomas, I felt entitled to a piece of the action.

I submitted my application to Goldman just months after Duke's class of 2008 set a powerful precedent: more graduates took jobs on Wall Street than anywhere else. And little has changed since the financial crisis—among the class of 2012, finance was the most popular industry for graduates of Harvard, Columbia, Duke, Georgetown, and even the University of Pennsylvania's *engineering* school. At Princeton, the number of graduates heading into finance was nearly three times higher than the number entering medical school.

* * *

My college experience was not supposed to unfold this way. When the coveted fat envelope landed in the mailbox of my family's Alabama home, I had never heard of Goldman Sachs. A bank was that one-story building across from a gas station where my mom deposited checks and I took more lollipops than I was supposed to.

Like many wide-eyed 18-year-olds with dreams of changing the world, I entered college with unbridled ambition, only to confront a harsh economic reality: undergraduate loans, the daunting cost of graduate degrees, and high unemployment. It is a common narrative among a generation that has come of age in a society that tells its youth that we can do or be anything but never mentions the suffocating price tag attached to our dreams.

I was, unknowingly, a prime target for the Wall Street recruiting machine. The loans I acquired to help pay for college, and my parents' frequent reminders of their own financial sacrifice, loomed large. And my dogged competitiveness, amplified on a campus of overachievers, predisposed me to the fight for the most coveted, selective opportunity on campus.

The college admissions guidebooks and campus tours—with all their talk of eccentric academic interests, liberal arts philosophies, and geographic and ethnic diversity—had neglected to mention that Wall Street's most powerful banks would invade campus during my junior year, dangling prestigious summer internships. Or that

3

the consulting industry, which exerts similar influence on campus, would do the same. I never planned to get sucked into the rat race. The odds, however, predicted that I would. The chase for these jobs is not just a defining characteristic of student life but an annual tradition, a rite of passage, and for many the climax of a college career.

That I had never expressed an interest in finance should have been strike one against my Wall Street dreams. The banks, however, would manage to convince me that my financial ignorance was irrelevant. The more recruiting events I attended, the more I heard the same reassuring line from Duke-graduates-turned-bankers: "When I arrived at Duke, I didn't even know what an investment bank *was*. I didn't even know the difference between a stock and a bond! And now, look at me—I work at (insert name here)!"

My strong aversion to the banking lifestyle was strike two. I had watched too many Wall Street–bound peers put their lives on hold and make significant sacrifices: friends, family, hobbies, and the careers they had expected to pursue. The idea of following in their workaholic footsteps was bleak, yet even this warning flag carried a caveat. The supersized egos, bonuses, and salaries make the drudgery seem thrilling. On a campus of overachievers, the 100-hour workweek has become an exhilarating challenge—the survival of the fittest. *If other students can handle it,* I reasoned, *why can't I?*

And then there was strike three: I launched my internship search in January 2009 while Wall Street was self-destructing and bringing the country down with it. There it is. Three strikes. Three reasons to abandon my short-lived investment banking fantasy. I should have bumped Wall Street off my list of potential employers, but I did not.

To understand how a rational student like me got swept up in an irrational phenomenon is to understand the forces that are influencing a generation and shaping the country's future leaders. This is not just *my* story. This is a story of college life that I have never heard anyone tell before.

* * *

Aidan stared at me, awaiting an answer. I looked my interviewer in the eye, sat up a little straighter, and cleared my throat. Then, with effortless delivery, I calmly and coolly tried to convince him why the hell I was doing this. I spoke of craving a challenge, thriving under pressure, and having a passion for numbers. I mentioned nothing of peer pressure, that I found finance utterly boring, or that I was intoxicated by the thought of earning a six-figure income before turning 23. Although Aidan would know I was lying, this was irrelevant. I had told him exactly what he wanted to hear, what he *needed* to hear. I proved I could feed the very lines that bankers repeat again and again to convince others, and themselves, that they did not, in fact, sell out.

When I completed my performance, Aidan's sly grin turned into a genuine smile. "Wonderful," he told me. "This is just wonderful to hear."

That I was so good at answering *Why finance?* was the very danger of this question. I had rehearsed and delivered my response so many times, and in such a persuasive fashion, that I had begun to believe it myself. Because Wall Street granted permission to tell a lie, I did not have to face the truth.

PART I

YEAR 1, SEMESTER 1

|||||||||||||||||||||||||||||||||||||||||||||||||||||||||||||||||||||||||||||||||||

*More than ever, American colleges and universities
seem to be in every business but education.*

—Jeffrey J. Selingo, editor at large for
The Chronicle of Higher Education

CHAPTER 1

The Fact That All of You Are Special Means That None of You Are

AUGUST 28, 2006, was my first day of college. It was one of those bright, sunny days in North Carolina when students play Frisbee on the quad, girls lay out picnic blankets and study in their bikinis, and Duke's stunning Gothic architecture is complemented by impeccable landscaping in its ornamental prime. Although students across the country begin their years in comparable weather, we took special pride in this picturesque opening, knowing there were plenty more days just like this one still to come. August 28 was the ideal welcome, a day of validation for the countless Duke students—me included—who had turned down Ivy League acceptances for the Ivy-equivalent school south of the Mason-Dixon, a place where the bright weather seems to feed students' boundless energy.

One week after my parents, my sister, and I had squeezed ourselves and most of my belongings into the family Honda for the eight-hour drive from Auburn, Alabama, to Durham, North Carolina, my alarm went off on the Monday morning that marked my new life as a college student. I sprang out of bed without the slightest temptation to hit the snooze button. My first class would not begin for another two hours, but the fear of doing something

9

wrong—oversleeping, getting lost, losing track of time over break-fast—was paralyzing enough to warrant an overly cautious schedule.

All of my morning essentials lay in a neat row on a desk not yet overtaken by papers and books. A shower caddy and fresh towel awaited the day's first stop at the communal bathroom across the hall. Next to this lay the outfit I had picked out the previous night and a tote bag that was already packed with new school supplies—a spiral notebook, a pen, a pencil, a highlighter, and the economics textbook that had cost a jaw-dropping $150.

After getting ready, I set out with a freshly printed class schedule in my left hand, a campus map in my right hand, and the sort of innocent confidence that only the freshest of freshmen can pull off. My college experience was in its honeymoon phase, a blissful time when terms like "weed-out course" and "problem set" were not yet part of my lexicon, and grades below "A" remained uncharted territory.

My map did not lead me to the grassy quad lined with Gothic-style buildings that housed classrooms and professors' offices. Instead, I headed in the opposite direction, away from campus's academic side. Somewhat skeptically, but with trust in my guide, I entered the student union, descended a staircase, passed the P.O. box-es and vending machines, and stumbled into a poorly lit corner of the building where the student union's cheerful sounds were muffled and its lively atmosphere was replaced by drab walls and tattered chairs. A glance at two oversized doors towering over me and a disappointed look back at my map assured me that I had, in fact, arrived at the home of "Economics 51D: Economic Principles,

Instructor Fincher, P. 10:05–11:20 MWF." I took a deep breath and, with a strong push, opened one of the doors and passed through this forbidding entrance to my first college class. My courses for that first semester—economics, Calculus III, Spanish, a mandatory writing course—were mostly a reflection of the subjects I had enjoyed and excelled at during high school. I had only a vague idea of what to study and even less clarity into what I wanted to do after college, but math classes had always been favorites of mine, and economics too seemed a strong contender, with its mix of theory, mathematics, and real-world applications.

I found myself in a large auditorium with stadium-style seating. I stood in one of two downward-sloping walkways that separated the rows of folding seats into three sections. Spiral notebooks rested on the desktops that folded upward from beneath the seats and barely provided us enough room for a piece of paper, let alone my enormous textbook. If an upperclassman had walked in, he would have laughed at a setting characteristic of the first day for a mostly freshmen course—not only was the auditorium nearly full 15 minutes before class began, but voices filled the air as students struck up conversations with the people sitting next to them.

From my perch overlooking the classroom, I readjusted the image of a liberal arts education that Duke's promotional literature had planted in my mind; the photos of students nestled in an intimate semicircle to facilitate lively discussion or sitting cross-legged on the quad clearly would not describe Economics 51D. Accepting the fact that my professor may never know my name—or even recognize my face—I gazed across the seats, looking for the best place to settle. But just when I was about to start down the aisle and claim a spot, I came to an abrupt halt.

My gaze rested on the person standing behind the podium, a broad-shouldered individual with the build of a football player. The short hair was bleached blond, smothered in gel, and spiked so dramatically that I wondered if he (or she?) assumed that the gathering horde of 18-year-olds had arrived in this auditorium not to learn how to calculate a firm's most profitable production level but to watch a has-been rocker perform. A hip emerged from behind the podium, followed by a sweeping floor-length skirt. When this woman turned around to pick up a stack of papers that rested on the stage, the assembling crowd noticed that hanging from her spiked hairdo and falling just below her shoulders was a long, thick rat tail.

"MINGDE!" A booming voice filled the auditorium, reaching me at the back with such force that I jumped.

"MINGDE, I cannot get the sound system to work!"

To my left, an Asian student fumbled anxiously with the auditorium's cumbersome sound board, a thousand switches and dials. He looked up at the sound of his voice—MINGDE!—and then stood, pressed his arms to his sides, and straightened, as if summoned by a military officer.

"MINGDE! The sound equipment!" It was a voice so deep and powerful that I questioned the need for a microphone.

"Coming!" The boy scurried past me and awkwardly barreled down the aisle.

I took a seat toward the back. I played with my pen and stole glances at the auditorium entrance, hoping that someone else would walk in, thank this woman for preparing the sound equipment, and commence the class. But I was looking at my professor. With a small microphone attached to her shirt and the sound equipment up and running, she filled the room with a voice that needed no amplification and a tone that made her version of a welcome sound more like a threat.

"This is Economics 51D, so I hope you are in the right place. I am Professor Fincher. I've taught this class before, but never to this many people." She scowled at a room that had filled to 450 students. The anger seemed directed at each and every one of us for making her job a little tougher.

"I don't really know how it's gonna work, because this class is just huge. So, you know"—Professor Fincher let out a big sigh and then, in a sardonic singsong voice, added—"it will be interesting to see what ha-a-a-ppens!"

Across the auditorium, heads swiveled and anxious glances were exchanged.

"We have a lot of teacher's assistants in this class," she continued, "but I want to introduce you to the two head TAs. Mingde and Harold, come here!"

The boy from earlier was joined on the stage by another.

"Mingde! What are your office hours?"

Cowering in front of Professor Fincher, who towered above him, Mingde attempted to say something but could not get it out.

"Do you even *have* office hours?"

I would later hear that the professor's father had been an NFL coach. Mingde was shaking in front of a woman who had acquired the demeanor of her father and the body type of his star linebackers.

As if smelling the boy's fear, she remarked, "This is not a test question."

"N-n-no," he stammered. "I don't have office hours. But I c-c-can, I can make them?"

"You can make them?" the professor shot back while twirling her rat tail around her finger. "Well, I would hope so."

"Yes, um, well, I can have my office hours on Mondays. Uh, and Wednesdays. From eight until nine in the morning."

"How nice! Eight in the morning. You will have office hours when no one will come!" I half expected Professor Fincher to ask Mingde to run laps around the auditorium or drop and do 20 push-ups. Instead, she turned her attention back to the freshmen, who watched in shock as our first classroom experience at Duke unfolded in a way nobody had anticipated.

We could have laughed at the exchange between Professor Fincher and Mingde as an outlet for our first-day jitters. Maybe, if this had been any class besides the one that initiated our college careers, there would have been something humorous about either of these wonderfully eccentric characters. But we could only envision ourselves in Mingde's shoes. It was too daunting to think that we, too, might incur Professor Fincher's wrath in the coming months, that we might accidentally provoke her.

"Let's talk about grades," Professor Fincher said, abruptly changing the subject. "I. Do. Not. Curve. Does everyone understand?"

Curving—like TAs and office hours—was a new concept to me. In high school, the grade on the paper was the grade that the teacher recorded. Tests were designed to be ace-able, a feat I could usually achieve. But at Duke, tests are frequently designed to be failed. The more challenging departments use their introductory courses to weed out the students. Hard tests achieve this goal, and then the professor manipulates the curve to salvage those who do "less badly." During midterm week each year, the freshmen dining hall is filled with naïve students flabbergasted over the chemistry exam where the average is a 55, or the biology exam where one-third of the students got below a 35. Although overachievers may cry when they first see a 65 written atop their midterm, if they look through their teary eyes and read the blackboard, they may see that all scores above 60 have been scaled to an A. Economics—the subject taught by Professor Fincher—qualifies within this "tougher" category. Although not as difficult as the sciences, it is considered one of Duke's "harder" majors, due to the math-intense requirements of Calculus III, statistics, and econometrics—on top of the mandatory calculus-based economics courses.

When Professor Fincher announced that she would not curve (ever), small gasps from those students who understood the importance of this college ritual filled the room.

"I do not curve because I do not believe in giving points away. We will have grades that are 100, and we will have grades that are 30." And when a class of former straight-A students heard the number 30, everyone now understood what was happening. But Professor Fincher had not finished.

"Twenty-five." Another gasp.

"Twenty." Silence.

"Eighteen."

* * *

On that first day gone wrong, Professor Fincher set in motion a first semester gone wrong and, with it, a downfall that would have implications I could not begin to comprehend. The pivotal moment of this ill-fated semester struck at its midpoint when a ringing phone interrupted my attempt at completing a math problem set that was just the first of many items on that night's cumbersome to-do list. I placed my pencil down and glanced at the phone to see that "Home" was calling. Up to this moment, I had successfully denied the eventuality of this call. It had been easier to pretend that this moment would not come than to wait for its arrival.

"Hello!" I answered cheerfully, though I knew on some level that picking up was a huge mistake. Just two months of college, it turned out, had been ample time to confirm that Professor Fincher's chilling introduction to college was not a quirk but an omen.

"Laura?" My dad's voice was uncharacteristically deep. That he posed my name as a question was the first indication of his mood.

"Yes."

Then, in the same stern tone came another statement presented as a question: "I'm calling about something your mother and I got in the mail today?" He paused. I said nothing, but then he asked another question, and this time it demanded a response. "Do you know what I'm talking about?"

Yes. Yes I do. Yes. I could think these words but not say them. If I said *Yes*, Dad would say, *Then tell me*, and I could not bring myself to explain the past two months.

So I held back the tears, stood up from my desk, and crawled into bed. As I waited for my dad to announce what had arrived in the mail, I wondered if I could handle his disappointment on top of everything else.

My downfall had come more quickly than I even thought possible. I had arrived at Duke feeling invincible, accepted into the school that *U.S. News & World Report* had ranked fifth in the country—tied with Stanford and placed higher than half of the Ivy League. I had walked away from a state ranked one of the country's worst in education for a school ranked one of the best.

Determined not to let Professor Fincher put a damper on my first semester, I had eagerly signed up for the mock-trial tryouts, ready to wow the judges just as I had done at Alabama's statewide competition, where I had racked up awards and was selected for the team we would send to the nationals. Within a week of my arrival at school, Duke's Mock Trial Club had assigned a case and placed me on a tryout team. I took comfort in the resemblance to high school. As my new Duke teammates and I sat around a conference table a few days before tryouts, I smiled at the memory of Sunday evenings when my high school teammates would gather around my family's kitchen table and dissect cases while my dog made circles around our feet and my mom prepared dinner.

My reminiscing was interrupted by a fidgety silence, and I looked up to find my teammates' eyes fixated on what rested in my hands, as if it were contraband.

"You are not planning to use notecards during the trial, are you?" one of them asked.

"Um, well, yeah."

17

They exchanged baffled looks, unsure of how to respond. Then, the guy sitting across from me cleared his throat and spoke on behalf of the group.

"We do not use notecards."

"Oh," I muttered, sliding my hands and the notecards they clutched beneath the table. "Really?"

"Yes." This time, they answered in unison, "Really."

One week earlier, we had been assigned a 125-page case to learn cover-to-cover. While adjusting to my first weeks of college and juggling an already-mounting workload, I assumed it acceptable to use notecards for the tryouts.

"Oh, I guess I misunderstood."

They looked at me, confused and disappointed.

Now nothing in the room reminded me of my high school days. We were not at a kitchen table but in a windowless classroom. There was neither laughing nor smiling, and my teammates held far too striking a resemblance to real lawyers.

At the following weekend's tryouts, I stumbled—sans notecards— over an opening statement, direct and cross-examinations, and objections. I wanted to blame the impossibly short one-week preparation period, but there was no excuse—my teammates breezed through the trial so effortlessly that I was tempted to resubmit my application to the Duke Admissions Committee with an asterisk next to my long list of mock-trial recognitions.

"You don't understand," I had attempted to explain to my father shortly after the tryouts in a phone conversation that foreshadowed the distressing one we would have two months later, "I humiliated myself. I was way out of my league."

"What do you mean?"

"These kids participated in hard-core mock-trial leagues that put Alabama's competition to shame. Their teams did not gather around kitchen tables once a week—they practiced every day! And remember how we would ask Mom what a term meant if we came across unfamiliar jargon?"

"Sure. The only time she put that law degree to use."

"Well, these kids did not ask a mother who never practiced law a day in her life what the definition of a word was! That was the extent of our 'professional' help. But Dad, these students, they had coaches."

"Coaches?"

"Coaches who were real lawyers."

"Oh! Well..." My dad stumbled, trying not to sound too impressed with this piece of information. "Well, sweetheart, I'm sure it didn't go as badly as you thought. You're just overreacting because you are upset. I watched you compete back in high school. I know talent when I see it, and you had real talent."

"But you didn't see these kids." And for the first time, I uttered the very phrase I would repeat again and again that semester: "It's not like it was in high school. It's just not the same at Duke."

"I still think you are being too hard on yourself."

"But Dad, you haven't even heard the most embarrassing part."

When the trial mercifully finished, I had stood with my team as the obvious weak link. I was so eager to bolt out of the room—and close the door on a chapter of my life that had come to an abrupt and disappointing end—that I did not realize that the president of the Mock Trial Club was offering feedback, and he was directing it at me.

"If you ever participate in a college mock-trial competition," he said sternly as he looked me over from top to bottom, "you will have to buy a new suit."

Everyone in the room turned to stare. Why was he even wasting his time—was it not clear that I would never compete in mock trial again? *Please don't make this any worse than it already is*, I silently begged him. But when I saw that he was firmly clutching a gavel as if it were his power source, I knew he would not relinquish authority until he had taken full advantage of this opportunity.

"Ideally, you should be wearing a pantsuit. But if you do wear a skirt suit," he warned, as his eyes and everyone else's fixated on my bare legs, "the skirt should fall below your knees. And you must wear stockings underneath."

I sheepishly tugged down on a skirt that fell just above my bare kneecaps as I stood in the same suit I had worn to countless high school competitions—the suit I had put on with such confidence that morning, feeling a rush of invincibility from my glory days. But as I remembered the mantra of my first two weeks at Duke—*nothing is like it was back home*—I understood why I was so out of place.

I had proudly worn my suit in competitions that were statewide, and in a state that is known neither for fashion nor for people who have enough money to pay for fashion, I now realized that the standards were unusually low. In my hometown of Auburn, the most upscale store is the Gap. There is not a Bloomingdale's or Nordstrom in all of Alabama, and only one city—located two hours from

Auburn—has a Macy's. Among students repulsed by the sight of notecards and trained by *real* coaches, it was foolish of me to assume that my outfit would fit in, when nothing else had.

The preparedness of my peers not only welcomed me to Duke's preprofessional culture but also suggested that this mentality had taken root long before many of them even set foot on campus. "And," the president continued, his gaze moving even lower until it reached my feet, "you *must* wear closed-toed shoes."

Standing rigidly in the makeshift courtroom as all eyes zoomed in on the girl who just did not get it, I was livid at myself for not even thinking twice about showing up at a Duke event in a suit from JCPenney's juniors section and shoes from Payless.

* * *

"Laura?" There it was again, my father's stern voice.

"Yes, Dad."

"I asked you a question. Do you know what your mother and I got in the mail today?"

"No," I lied, "no, I don't." I braced for impact.

My dad uttered the phrase I had been dreading, drawing out his delivery with a slow and forceful voice: "Duke sent us your midterm grades."

Don't say it, I thought. *I cannot listen to it. Please don't say it.*

"It says here"—I heard a piece of paper forcefully being unfolded on the other end, and I envisioned my dad pulling out his glasses and holding the paper taut, even though he had already memorized exactly what was on it—"that you have a C in economics and a D in math."

Silence.

"A C and a D, Laura! Did you know about this?"

"Yes." Another lie. I had not known what the grades would be, just that they would be bad. I did not mention my relief upon hearing that my math professor had graciously granted me a D when, after I failed the midterm, the grade should have been an F.

"You're almost failing!" The tears finally broke through and would not stop. *Failing.* A word that had never been part of my vocabulary now seemed to define my college experience.

After the mock-trial catastrophe, I had picked myself up and tried to find a different extracurricular activity. But by the end of my first month at Duke, I had invested hours upon hours in interviews, applications, and tryouts for opportunities that—one by one—rejected me. In the classroom, my endless hours of studying were clearly not yielding results, either.

"A D in math?" Although I held the phone a few inches away from my ear, I had no difficulty hearing.

"Yes."

"But you are *so* good at math."

"No, Dad. I *was* good at math."

Two summers earlier, I had aced a Calculus II class at Auburn University. Calculus III at Duke should not have been much different, yet it was. My Auburn professor had graded just like the one at Duke—the curve was strict, designed to sort through the students unable to handle a class required for engineering, math, and science majors. But at Duke, the bell curve had shifted so far to the right that I now fell on the far left of its tail.

"No," my father shouted, "no! You *are* good at math."

I had rarely angered him this way before. I now trembled at an unfamiliar voice.

"You got a perfect 800 on the SAT math section, for crying out loud!"

"Yeah, well, I'm sure a lot of others in this class did, too, and the professor cannot give As to us all."

"So? Then just be one of those students who gets an A."

There was a long silence on the line. Finally, after my father grilled me about study habits and falsely accused me of skipping class and partying hard, we hung up.

My dad's anger and my over-the-top tears were fueled by something neither of us could bear to admit. The elephant in the room that had escalated a tense conversation into a screaming match was money. Although my parents—my father a professor and my mother a social worker—had supported my goal of attending a top school, it was my dream and not theirs. My parents were literally empty nesters; not only had my older sister and I left home, but we took their nest egg with us. Instead of reaping the benefits of a lifetime of hard work and frugality, they were pinching every penny to make the tuition payments every six months. My sister and I shouldered the burden, too, accumulating tens of thousands of dollars in student loans. All for the promise of one of the best educations the country could offer.

It was my formidable economics professor who reinforced my worst fear—that at Duke, I would be average at best. Shortly after the explosive conversation with my dad, Professor Fincher sent an e-mail to the entire class, a message that would become infamous among Duke's class of 2010. When the note landed in my inbox, I could hear the professor's deep voice reading each word with a fiery passion that was neglected when describing marginal cost curves and instead reserved for demeaning her students:

> . . . You must learn that the playing field has now changed.
> All of you are smart, or you would not be here. This makes
> the competition and the metrics much stiffer. This also means
> that while you were "special" in your previous life, the fact
> that all of you are special means that none of you are. . . .

Maybe she was right. Perhaps I was not smart enough to take advantage of all that my parents were paying for. I had been left with no choice but to reevaluate my potential major (economics), minor (mathematics), and extracurricular activities (too many to list). With each disappointment, I watched as my family's investment suffered write-off after write-off until its value approached a number dangerously close to zero. The number $200,000, the rough cost of my college education, took on a life of its own, weighing on me and growing heavier with each passing day. It seemed ever less likely that anything I accomplished at Duke could justify such a hefty expense.

Or, at least, this is how I felt until I made a fascinating discovery, a revelation that would strike at my most vulnerable time and change everything. Simply by coming to Duke, I had apparently made myself a target for the elite investment banks. And while a term like *investment bank* meant little to me, the concept of earning a six-figure income at age 22 meant a lot. At these places, at these investment banks, it seemed that everyone played by a different set of rules—a more appealing set of rules. For my family, $200,000 may have been a lot of money. But I could go to a place where this was mere pocket change.

YEAR 1, SEMESTER 1

The College Board likes to say that the average debt is "only" $27,650. What the Board doesn't say is that when personal circumstances go wrong, as can happen in a recession, interest, late payment penalties, and other charges can bring the tab up to $100,000. Those going on to graduate school, as upwards of half will, can end up facing twice that . . . [students are] veering away from jobs they may really want—like inner-city teaching or family practice medicine—for others better suited to meet repayment schedules.

—Andrew Hacker and Claudia Dreifus,
   "The Debt Crisis at American Colleges,"
   The Atlantic, August 17, 2011

CHAPTER 2

Where Did You Summer?

THE ATTRACTION TO banking sneaked up on me. There was no *aha!* moment, only a collection of observations and experiences— some striking, but most mundane—that subtly accumulated until I simply knew that I wanted a career in finance, although I had little idea how it had become so appealing or, more important, *why.*

The seed was planted early in my college career, shortly after Professor Fincher's ominous welcome to Duke. It was during that first month of my freshman year that I noticed an interesting shift of wardrobe among my peers. On a campus brimming with jeans, hoodies, frumpy backpacks, and the occasional pajama bottoms, even the most unsuspecting of freshmen would be surprised by the sudden influx of peers who sported full suits and carried briefcases. Although I knew the professional dress was related to the job search, I did not know *which* jobs warranted such impressive attire so early in the school year, and I did not care. Nevertheless, it was impossible not to draw some inference from the number of students who brazenly broke the campus dress code in such remarkable fashion. I assumed that these jobs, whatever they may be, must be special if such a sizable portion of the student body would dress up like *that* for employers so proactive and so confident in their stability that they could recruit talent almost one full year before their advertised positions would begin.

My initial musing, no matter how insignificant it seemed at the time, was correct. The suits made an impression on me with good reason. There are, I would learn, two industries that heavily recruit so early in the school year, and it is these two fields that unequivocally make up the holy grail of the job search. The first, the undisputed top dog, is finance. No longer the broad term used to describe the industry that employs the manager of your local credit union or the teller at your bank, "finance" carries one distinct meaning at colleges like Duke. Here, working in finance means working on Wall Street. "Banking" is virtually interchangeable with "finance." In campus lingo, to work at a bank means to work at an *investment* bank—a financial powerhouse such as Goldman Sachs, J.P. Morgan, or UBS.[1] An investment bank (more commonly known as an *i-bank*) is *not* a building with an ATM outside, tellers inside, and a drive-through window on the side. Although some i-banks have commercial branches, most positions available to top students are located at a bank's headquarters, usually in a Manhattan skyscraper where large trading floors, merger and acquisition deal teams, and underwriting and research operations are housed.

Finance jobs are often considered the most popular and flashiest of opportunities, but they face a rival in the consulting industry. Like banking, consulting was a career path I had never thought much about before arriving at college. I did not know what consultants

---

1. During the 2008 financial crisis, many traditional investment banks reclassified themselves as "bank holding companies." However, this new title is mostly considered a technicality. The term "investment bank" is a moniker unlikely to disappear.

do, other than, well, consult—yet another nebulous term, but one so professional sounding that I assumed consultants were specialists or industry veterans, not 22-year-olds. My ignorance mattered little. On a campus targeted by the preeminent consultancies, it did not take long to catch on. Consulting firms are entirely separate from Wall Street. Consultants are hired by companies to solve a problem—any type of company facing any type of problem. Although I had never heard of firms like the Boston Consulting Group (BCG) or Accenture, I *had* heard of their clients—the companies that make up the Fortune 500 list. For a Duke graduate, there is nothing glamorous about getting a job at the headquarters of a company like Allstate or Walmart, but it sure is glamorous to earn far more money working for the firms that work for those companies.

So there it is. Finance and consulting. I would not understand their nuances during my first semester, or even my first year, at Duke. But I would learn enough to be intrigued, enough to want to know more.

Seeing the plethora of suits had piqued my interest, a dangerous curiosity on a campus where even the slightest inclination toward a banking or consulting career is subject to enough positive reinforcement to transform that inclination into infatuation. And so began the process—without my authorization or even awareness—in which the terms *investment banking* and *consulting* became fixtures in my vocabulary. Unfamiliar names like Bain, Lazard, and Bear Stearns rolled off my tongue with a fluency I had not studied to attain. No professor ever quizzed me on this; there was no *U.S. News & World Report* ranking equivalent to pore over. The information seeped in, anecdote by anecdote.

"I am working for Morgan Stanley," I might hear a senior say—en route to class or passing through the dining hall—each letter sharply enunciated to convey pride for this elite investment bank.

"Oh, well, Matt got an offer from a private equity firm," another would report, facial expression wavering between jealousy and admiration.

I began to pick up subtle signals, shifts in tone. I noticed the stark contrast between an elated "I got a McKinsey offer!" and the middling "I'm going to the Advisory Board Company." In some cases, I watched seniors awkwardly avoid sharing a name because the bank or consulting firm whose offer they had accepted was considered low in prestige. I had thought a job offer was a job offer—if it came from a campus recruiter and arrived before graduation. Apparently not.

Internships were also coveted. When students asked, "Where did you summer?" they meant, "What bank or consultant did you intern for?" Until this point, the verb "to summer" was something I had heard only on celebrity reality shows when referring to the Hamptons or a villa in the South of France.

It was irrelevant that names like McKinsey and terms like "to summer" meant nothing to me. The body language told me everything I needed to know. With each overjoyed grin or muddled response, it became clearer that an entire hierarchy—not just professional, but *social*—had arisen around the job search.

Hard proof came in the form of Todd Erby. He was the stereotypical Duke nice guy—brilliant, generous, a wonderful conversationalist, and unsuccessful with women. Todd was the only senior in his fraternity who remained a virgin, something that his brothers never let him forget. His shyness and average looks were sure to make him coveted husband material in 10 years, not hook-up material for college girls in search of a campus big shot. I met Todd during the first semester of my freshman year, when I became friends with one of his younger fraternity brothers. Toward the end of that fall semester, I noticed a puzzling attitude shift as Todd—the virgin and nerd who had gone through his Duke career largely unnoticed—acquired a new persona. The scarlet V on Todd's chest had been replaced by a more powerful symbol: GS. Todd had received an offer from Goldman Sachs, the most esteemed i-bank, and with movie-arc timing, a beautiful blond girl from a wealthy family appeared on his arm.

Todd's sudden stardom may sound juvenile—and it couldn't have seemed sillier to me at the time—but it was fascinating. To a lost freshman who thought the lows couldn't get any lower, there was nothing more seductive than the idea of living the high life. During a first semester of college that was as perplexing as it was upsetting, the sales pitch for the finance and consulting industries resonated with me like an infomercial touting the latest get-rich-quick scheme. The testimonials may have sounded too good to be true, yet transformations like Todd's occurred before my eyes. The promises may have seemed grandiose, but I learned that the salaries really were *that* big.

Wall Street and the top consulting firms are a brainy kid's Hollywood or NFL. The glamorous lifestyle seemed like the natural place to set my sights—the panacea for my financial woes, low confidence, and nobody status. Sure, it appeared unlikely that a D student like me could achieve something so lofty, but when has reality ever prevented someone from dreaming of hitting it big?

YEAR 2, SEMESTER 2

The big money that can be had in finance attracts some of the brightest minds. And when financial services were helping to drive the economy, sending the cream of the academic crop to Wall Street seemed to make sense. After the last few years of financial crisis, though, some people are asking whether it's worth it for the graduates and for the country.

> —"Is a Job on Wall Street Still Worth It?"
> American Public Media's *Marketplace*,
> May 25, 2010

CHAPTER 3

Campus Royalty

ON A WINTER morning with temperatures hovering slightly above freezing, I had an appointment with Duke's very own Wall Street superstar. I was just a sophomore, but for the next 15 minutes I owned the time of a woman who had served as a trader and an executive director at Goldman Sachs. Despite a Wharton MBA, a Duke PhD, and a bachelor's degree from Oxford, this academic and industry powerhouse is known on campus simply as Emma. Every campus has its celebrities, and Emma is one of Duke's—an insider who offers a gold mine of resources to the students lucky enough to earn her respect.

Emma is the linchpin between Duke and Wall Street. Although Duke already sends large numbers of students into finance, Emma's mission is to make the school an even stronger incubator of financial geniuses. Her work is multifaceted. On Wall Street, she maintains close relationships with the top banks to ensure that they grant Duke the coveted distinction of a "target school." At Duke, she helps students hone their financial know-how so they can convince the banks that even though the Ivy League colleges are more accessible, a school 500 miles from Manhattan is well worth the visit.

To meet her goal of making Duke an even more finance-friendly school, Emma founded the Financial Education Partnership to train students in financial techniques, launched a financial immersion program that places students in Manhattan for a semester, and created a mentoring network to connect students with Wall Street big shots. She teaches some of the few classes offered about the financial markets and, just months before I graduated, spearheaded the effort to create a finance minor and a finance concentration within the economics major—a move that will only shepherd more students into the field and more recruiters to campus.

Duke even has Emma to thank for recruiting events like the Finance Madness Game Show, a *Jeopardy*-style competition that Deutsche Bank sponsored a few years ago. The coveted i-bank not only sent its bankers to attend the mock game show but even flew the winner to New York for a tour of its trading floor and an interview for its summer internship. Finance Madness was just one of the many financial competitions Emma transformed from a laughable display of geekiness into an event that is sponsored by a major i-bank and accompanied by a glamorous prize for the winner.[2]

Emma is one of many forces making a finance career so accessible, prominent, and appealing that students get hooked as freshmen or sophomores before they are exposed to alternatives. Leaving Duke as a banker has never been easier.

With some trepidation, I entered Emma's office at the start of the second semester of my sophomore year. I was preparing to declare economics as my major, but this had little to do with my decision

---

2. Other colleges offer similar finance competitions.

to meet Emma. At that time at Duke, the economics major still maintained a heavy liberal arts focus. The classes were primarily theoretical and had little, if anything, to do with the financial markets. (This would change following Emma's establishment of the finance concentration and minor.)

I met with Emma because it was, I assumed, a good time to begin considering a career. Due to its on-campus prominence, banking seemed an option worth exploring, and despite my brush with failure as a freshman, it was now a feasible option. Those disastrous midterm grades had served as a wake-up call, and I had assessed my study habits and trashed the high school methods that could not cut it at Duke. The reform paid off, elevating my C to a B and my D to a B-minus, and it yielded an A and an A-minus in my other classes. My missteps were salvageable, and after two more semesters, I had a decent—but not great—GPA.

I had never met Emma before, but I expected that a woman who had climbed the ranks on a male-dominated trading floor would have acquired a stern, unfeminine, and emotionless demeanor. Or she might be the stereotypical corporate bitch—attractive, meticulously put together, and catty. Whichever category Emma fell into, I was prepared to be intimidated.

But I almost wondered if I had walked into the wrong office as I shook hands with a woman for whom "high-powered, cutthroat financial mogul" would be the last phrase to enter one's mind. This was a pixie of a woman, a petite gamine, with hair that needed to be brushed and soft features not highlighted by makeup. Emma wore a pale blue blouse with white buttons down the middle, a flimsy collar, and an untucked-in tail that now hung carelessly over unfitted pants. Her simplicity and calm nature reminded me less of an aggressive trader and more of a dedicated yet overworked mother. I suddenly relaxed. This would be doable.

But then Emma started talking, and everything changed.

She began with a simple question: "So, Laura, tell me why you are here."

"Well, I know that finance is a common career path for students, but I don't know too much about the field yet. There's still plenty of time to figure it all out, I know, so I'm hoping you can tell me more about the opportunities for someone who is considering the industry."

I smiled, pleased with the informative yet concise opening. I had expected Emma to respond with, *You have taken a great first step. You shouldn't be worrying too much about these things because you are just a sophomore!* And then, I had imagined, she would pull out a clipboard and say, *So, let's start with a list of things you can do to become prepared.*

But Emma looked unimpressed. There was not a trace of the warm smile that I had expected, given her motherly and nurturing appearance.

"What are you doing right now to become financially aware?" she demanded.

"Well, I stay on top of the news and—"

"Do you read the *Journal?*"

"The *Wall Street Journal?*" I clarified.

A stunned look, then, across her desk, she stared at me scornfully, as if I had insulted one of her children. She cleared her throat and in a stern voice uttered four words that I will never forget: "There's only one *Journal.*"

A painful silence filled the room as I recognized the gravity of Emma's statement and my own slip-up.

Finally, with a trembling voice, I attempted to appease her: "Um, not every day, but yes, I do read it often." It was my first lie to a Goldman Sachs banker.

Emma looked down again, and this time she shook her head, disappointed. "You must read the *Journal*. Every. Single. Day." She carefully enunciated these last words like a military commander.

"OK. I'll start doing that."

"The students who will get the internships have been reading the *Journal* every day since their freshman year." Emma paused, and for the first time, a smile surfaced. But it was a mocking one. "Sounds like you have a lot of catching up to do."

The race had already begun, and apparently I was the only one to have missed the starting shot fired at the beginning of freshman year. Emma was the angry coach who made me feel like the out-of-shape kid running at the back of the pack.

"Where is the S&P now?" Emma snapped at me.

"Um, the S&P?" I knew that the S&P was a collection of 500 large stocks, but that was the beginning and end of my knowledge. "I'm sorry. I don't know." I looked down at the notebook that lay open on my lap. Written on the top page was a list of the questions I had prepared for our meeting. I had worried that there would not be enough time to get through all of them in the 15-minute slot.

Now I closed my notebook, realizing that there would not be an opportunity to ask a single one.

"What about the Dow? Tell me where the Dow is."

I hesitated, and before I could mutter an excuse for not knowing this one either, Emma snidely remarked, "I guess I shouldn't even bother asking about gold. Or the dollar."

As I sat across from Emma, berated by the woman to whom I had come for mentoring, I wondered how I had gotten here, inquiring about an industry I knew so little about. I thought back to the simple question that I had asked my career adviser one week before meeting with Emma.

* * *

Trevor was the career adviser at Duke who specialized in business-sector jobs, even though he was no older than 30 and could not have had much, if any, experience in his professed field of expertise. When I had met with him the week before, I posed a basic question.

"I've heard a lot of buzz about finance and consulting. But I'm interested in other business opportunities. Is there anything else in the business world available for Duke students?"

Trevor did not seem to hear the last part of my question. Like a marriage counselor who springs into action upon hearing the phrase "no sex in the marriage," my career adviser perked up at the cue word "finance." There was no weighty discussion about options within finance or alternatives to finance. Instead, he opened Power-Point on his computer and began his sales pitch.

The dreadful PowerPoint presentation that I sat through reminded me of the brochures whose titles I had browsed while waiting for the doctor one day at the student health clinic. The cover of each pamphlet featured a smiling teenager playing catch or laughing with friends. He or she always looked surprisingly happy, even though, according to the title, this teenager had a serious problem: *So, you have herpes? . . . So, you think you may be pregnant?*

When the presentation, which should have been called "So, You're Thinking of Becoming a Banker?" was finally finished, Trevor turned to me and asked seriously, "So, what do you think? Does finance sound like a good fit for you?"

"Um, I guess," I replied. "I am hardworking, I'm good with numbers, and I like a fast-paced environment—just like the slides said. I guess I should be a banker!" Trevor didn't notice the sarcasm. He smiled, pleased with his superb diagnostic skills. I wondered if there were any Duke students who did not, as the PowerPoint asked, crave a challenging environment, an opportunity to quickly climb a firm's ranks, and generous compensation.

I sat through a second painful narration by Trevor, this time a presentation that should have been titled "So, You're Thinking of Becoming a Consultant?"

And then I revived my original question.

"What about other business fields? You know, sectors other than finance and consulting?" I hoped Trevor would discuss opportunities with employers like Johnson & Johnson, Coca-Cola, Apple, Disney, Nike, or GE—multinational companies with diverse operations. This was what "business" meant to *me*. But to Trevor and to Duke and many of its peer institutions, "business" has morphed into a synonym for the two narrow fields of finance and consulting.

Trevor stumbled, unsure of what to say because, apparently, there was not a PowerPoint presentation to answer the question.

He finally offered, "Well, if you want a career in business, an internship is a great place to start. Let me show you how to find one." He then mercifully closed PowerPoint and opened a Web browser. He gave me a tour of the Career Center's website and then sent me on my way.

I had come for career counseling, and instead I received two PowerPoint presentations and a Web tutorial. That was when I realized the great irony of the young employees who are put in charge of Duke students' career plans. Trevor had become a business-sector career adviser before acquiring any experience in the business world; maybe, I mused, he had become a career adviser because the business world would not hire him.

And yet he had done a terrific job, for the finance industry. His message was clear: if I wanted a paid internship—the only type I could afford—banks were the only business that would pay. *So, why not go for it?* I thought. The banks seemed to be worth a shot.

I had walked out of Trevor's office and, shortly after, into Emma's.

* * *

Emma was not letting up. "Tell me the names of the three banks that have announced major write-downs in the past week." She was referring to a financial system that was showing the beginning signs of collapse. It seemed that every week a different bank dominated headlines with news that ominously predicted the decline of the industry's health.

"Merrill Lynch," I muttered. I had seen the headlines and read some of the articles (in the *Times,* not the *Journal*). But as Emma glared, the names of the other banks escaped me.

"Uh," I said, stalling for time. We sat in silence. Emma looked at her watch.

"Oh! UBS?" I finally spat out in a high-pitched voice that trailed off and revealed my uncertainty.

"Those two are correct, but you still missed one. This has been *major* news. There is no excuse for not knowing this."

She continued, "Have you received the e-mails or seen the flyers about the different finance events that I host? The competitions? The finance lecture series? The recruiting workshops?"

"Yes, I've seen the e-mails."

"All right." Emma breathed a sigh of relief and permitted a slight smile to creep upon her face, optimistic that we would finally make progress. But I stared at the ground, ashamed, unable to return the smile because I knew exactly what was coming.

"So, have you participated in any of these activities?"

"No," I answered sheepishly, wondering why I would have signed up for the Corporate Valuation Case Study Competition or written an essay about equity futures when I did not even know what corporate valuation or equity futures were.

"Well, you asked about internships that are available to sophomores." I looked up, hopeful.

"As a matter of fact, there are a few options available, but they are very competitive." Emma paused and then repeated, "Very. Competitive."

"I see."

"Sophomore-year internships are much more competitive than the internships for juniors."

"I know."

"To get one of these internships, you have to do more. The students you will compete against have participated in the case competitions. *They* come to the finance lectures. *They* come to the workshops. *They* read the *Journal*."

"I understand."

"*They* have been developing an interest in finance since their freshman year, and some even before that, in order to best position themselves for a top internship slot."

"I see that now," I told Emma, recognizing that she and her Wall Street peers expected liberal arts students to declare a career before even declaring a major. "I had thought that getting started as a sophomore was early enough. Now I know that I have a lot of catching up to do."

I stood up, shook Emma's hand, and walked out the door, wondering why she had not just saved herself a few breaths by saying, "*They* are better than you."

In that moment, I believed that they *were* better than me. And I was bitter. I wanted to blame my high school guidance counselor for setting a terrible example by not discussing colleges until my senior year—leading me to think that sophomore year was a great head start for jobs. Or I could blame my career adviser, Trevor, whose PowerPoint presentations neglected to mention the S&P, the *Journal*, and the intimidating personalities like Emma who are the norm in the industry.

I walked out of Emma's office angry, but I should have been grateful. She offered a glimpse into finance, an industry that values curtness and does not, under any circumstances, put up with someone who cannot play by the rules. And Emma delivered a second lesson, a lesson that goes unmentioned in freshmen orientation and unspoken by most students, faculty members, parents, and admissions advisers because to say it aloud is to undermine everything we want to believe a liberal arts college stands for. Emma admitted the truth—that the first years of college are neither a chance to explore nor a reprieve from high school's manufactured and over-hyped sprint to the ivy-covered finish line. Whether you are bound for Wall Street, medical school, law school, or many other career destinations, there is little time to catch your breath. On day one, the clock resets, and this time the stakes are higher, the posturing begins earlier, and the competitors are savvier.

This lesson is essential for success in college life, yet there is a major divide between those who know it from the start, those who learn it just in time, and those who do not find out until it is too late. With the rare courage to speak the truth, Emma offered *me* the opportunity to learn it just in time.

* * *

Emma warned that my peers—the ones who monitor the Dow and woo bankers at finance-themed game shows—would outmuscle me because even the most cursory of glances at our differing backgrounds indicated that they would. It is not just on elite campuses but at many colleges that a significant portion of the student body hails from achievement-obsessed suburbia, where SAT test-prep classes are de rigueur, private admissions counselors charge thousands and sometimes tens of thousands, and parents spare no expense to nurture talents that will be dropped as soon as the acceptance letter arrives. Many of my peers had been primed for superstardom at every turn, and it is this mentality that has earned my generation the label of the entitled generation—if a child displays even a sliver of talent, a private coach will be hired to develop it; if she shows the slightest deviation from excellence, a therapist, tutor, or Adderall will be sought to fix it.

That *my* upbringing was nothing of the sort was irrelevant. On a campus like Duke's, this culture reappears and even intensifies among those who emerged victorious from the selective college application process. My well-trained classmates had begun grooming their résumés on day one, initiating a race that all must join, lest we fall behind the pack. For those raised to view the college search as a game, it is natural to view the job search in the same light.

The most successful recruiters *get* this. They understand that our hypercompetitiveness leaves us scrambling for one-upmanship. So they pull out all the stops in a relentless attempt to outshine one another and prove supremacy. In other words, the students are not the only ones seeking an edge. In the latest manifestation of this absurd power struggle, banks (but in this case, usually not consulting firms) begin recruiting students as sophomores. They offer sophomore-only paid internship programs over the summer, and during the school year they host one- or two-day-long educational and networking programs at their Manhattan offices. (All travel expenses are covered, of course, for those accepted to the exclusive overnight events.) They know that if we are offered opportunities to build our résumés, we will not just apply but commit ourselves so fully that we will mistake our desire to win the race for a desire to attain whatever it is that we are chasing.

These employers intensify a hit-the-ground-running frenzy that is already excessive on competitive campuses. Every summer matters. Because GPA is a crucial measure, every class matters. The message is loud and clear: it is never too early to start the job hunt, and it is never too early to gain a head start on your peers.

With Emma's help, I understood the urgency of this message. And it sounded an awful lot like an ultimatum. To be considered for the most accessible career path that my school offered, I would have to enter the race immediately. Otherwise, it would be difficult to find my footing—not just on the paths leading to Wall Street but on those leading nearly everywhere else too. I thought of my peers who had already identified paths that would make parents proud and peers envious, trajectories for which preparation had begun swiftly, strategically, and with all the excess of an overachiever. I, too, needed to be working toward something, to be running in front of the pack—or at least not falling too far behind. And to exclude myself from the industry that hired more of my peers than any other seemed limiting, irresponsible, and borderline reckless.

YEAR 2, SEMESTER 2

Students now identify more with CEOs of corporations or hedge funds than they do with the figure lecturing behind the podium. As professors focus on their research, and students worry about securing career opportunities, both sides become increasingly disinterested in the classroom. . . . Students take less time to explore intellectually, worried more about carving out a tangible path for their futures.

—Elizabeth S. Auritt and Delphine Rodrik, "The Fall of Academics at Harvard," *The Harvard Crimson*, February 28, 2013

CHAPTER 4

Good, but Not Good Enough

On a typical day, the Bryan Center is lightly populated. Students meander through in Duke hoodies or leggings tucked into Ugg boots. They carry lunch, textbooks, or mail just picked up from a P.O. box. The sounds are refreshing and youthful: pop music emanating from eateries, the turning of pages as students study or read the campus paper, and an uneven but heartening blend of free-flowing conversation and laughter.

But on January 15, 2008, I hardly recognized my student union. The music was drowned out by uncharacteristically loud, and forced, conversation. Blue hoodies were replaced by black blazers, leggings by slacks, and Uggs by heels and dress shoes. If any overworked students had pulled an all-nighter, no one could tell. Guys' faces were clean-shaven and the girls' were made up. Hair was brushed and styled. We all held the same thing—a padfolio adorned with a gold or silver Duke crest that glistened when the light hit at the right angle. And even though most of us had come from class or would head there after, backpacks were replaced by briefcases and Longchamp bags—the pricey leather-trimmed totes that are popular among professional women.

On this special day, Wall Street came to *us*. The five largest investment banks—Goldman Sachs, Morgan Stanley, Bear Stearns,

Merrill Lynch, and Lehman Brothers—were only a handful of the financial firms in attendance that morning. For them, a rocky 2007 had just come to an end. Their shareholders had lost more than $80 billion, and three of these five banks had posted the worst quarterly losses in their history. Nearly 5,000 jobs were being eliminated among the five employers. Nevertheless, at the year's end, these five banks alone had paid their employees $39 *billion* in bonuses.

To the crowds that came to the Bryan Center, the thought of earning a piece of this pie bridged the unspoken financial divide between the indebted student who was desperate to pay off her loans and her privileged classmate who was unable to imagine a life that did not provide the same amenities she was accustomed to.

For students today, it is tough to stomach the thought of taking on the average $167,000 debt load of a medical student, shelling out $50,000 a year for a master's degree, or committing at least five years to earn a PhD. These daunting postgraduate costs are often piled atop undergraduate debt, which in 2012 averaged about $27,000. No wonder our priorities are skewed.

Wall Street becomes a short-term fix, and once you are there, it is tough to leave. In 2011, *Bloomberg* reported that a banker with 10 years of experience specializing in mergers would earn $2 million a year—more than 10 times the salary of an equally experienced cancer researcher or aerospace engineer. And these financiers often get their start at the very firms that now populated the Bryan Center.

Yes, recruiting season was upon us. There were all the telltale signs. Red Solo cups had disappeared from Facebook profile pictures, the stock of padfolios was depleted in the bookstore, and class attendance had begun to dwindle. Each of the two career fairs ushers in a semiannual invasion in which employers colonize Duke and dominate student conversations and anxieties for months to come.

The first career fair of a school year occurs in September, about three weeks after students return from summer break and at least nine months before they will begin work at the jobs being advertised. This fair targets seniors (though this does not dissuade juniors, sophomores, and even freshmen from attending events to network). By most students' sophomore year, they already have the goal of avoiding this recruiting season for full-time jobs by landing an internship as a junior, receiving a job offer that summer, and embarking on a worry-free senior year.

The second fair of the school year is the one I attended as a sophomore, shortly after my disheartening meeting with Emma. After passing out full-time offers to seniors in the fall, employers return in January, this time looking for interns. At many of the booths, if a jobless senior approaches, the representative will likely turn away this "undesirable"—that ship has already sailed.

I stood in the Bryan Center looking down pathways cluttered with foot traffic. Tables lined both sides of the walkways and were shoved into every unoccupied nook and cranny. Each table, or booth, had a banner draped over the front, a pile of branded knickknacks on top, and one or two representatives standing behind. And this was only on the first of the three floors hosting employers. Among the dark-suited students who roamed the Bryan Center and waited patiently, if stiffly, to meet the guests of honor, our differences were relegated to the black text on the pieces of white paper pressed into the side flaps of our padfolios. Put together, our résumés read like an encyclopedia. Students in my graduating class alone hailed from 46 states and 41 countries. Our talents were impressive and quirky. We boasted math geniuses, Olympic athletes, and students who spoke tribal languages.

But at the career fair, you would never know this.

That day, Duke students were so vanilla that a passerby would never guess that among us were many Cameron Crazies—students who helped make Duke's basketball team famous by painting their bodies blue, donning blue wigs, and inventing some of the cleverest cheers in college sports while screaming like maniacs in the stands. Some of these obsessed fans had awakened that morning on a surface even less comfortable than a dorm mattress: the ground in 35-degree weather. This is part of "tenting," the annual phenomenon in which students whose parents are paying thousands in housing fees live in a makeshift tent-village for up to two months before the home game against archrival North Carolina. The morning of the career fair, some of these students rolled out of sleeping bags, escaped to the warm refuge of their dorms, took hot showers, and stepped into tailored suits—completing the transformation from rugged sports fanatic to primped professional. They placed into briefcases all the necessities for a day of classes, job searching, and extracurricular activities. Like those profiled in the Duke "view book" that arrives in the mailboxes of high-performing high school juniors each fall, the quintessential student seems to do it all, effortlessly.

I blended into the Bryan Center crowd. Mostly. I had retired the infamous JCPenney suit from my mock-trial disaster for a slight upgrade. The week before the fair, I had borrowed a friend's car for an emergency trip to a Durham mall. Although my mom likely would have pitched in for a nice suit, I did not want to ask her, since I did not yet have an internship, let alone an interview. So I assigned myself a $100 budget with the money from my school-year job and bought a simple black suit. I was proud of my purchase; it was not revolutionary, but the first of many baby steps. Unlike my mock-trial skirt suit, this one had pants. It was not from JCPenney but from the discount women's store New York and Company. And while I still wore Payless shoes, my newest were closed-toed.

I had completed one other prerequisite before attending the fair. My brand-new padfolio—the leather-bound folder whose interior includes a legal pad and an assortment of flaps to hold business cards, résumé copies, and so on—was the cheapest available at the campus bookstore. The cover was a dreary gray instead of glossy black, and my Duke crest was a dull silver instead of a shimmery gold. Because I owned neither a Longchamp nor any of the professional bags that so many Duke women carried, I squeezed my keychain into one of the padfolio's side pockets, creating a sizable bulge that prevented the folder from closing neatly.

"Looking gooooooood," I heard a familiar voice say. I turned around to see my boyfriend, Alex, approaching me. His gaze tracked my figure, hugged by the black suit, from top to bottom and back to the top again. His eyes grew wide—as if pleasantly surprised or even shocked—at the sight of my blond hair, which I had straightened and let down so that it fell just below my shoulders and framed a face brightened by makeup. He lifted his index finger and twirled it slowly in hopes that my body would do the same.

"No," I said meekly. I stood in place, defying Alex's request as my shoulders slouched inward and my arms fell across my body as if covering myself in the cold. I wondered why I still felt self-conscious around him.

"Maybe after breakfast, then," Alex said, grabbing my hand and leading me down the stairs to get something to eat at one of the few unoccupied corners of the Bryan Center. He was a junior—one year above me and a prime target of that day's fair—but he did not wear a suit. Nor did he have a pile of MCAT, LSAT, or GRE prep books piled atop a desk in his dorm room. And it was for this reason that Alex carried himself with even more confidence that morning, as if looking down on his misguided peers, certain that he was better than this.

"I'll be right over there," I announced, pointing at an empty table as I slipped away to grab it while Alex waited in line for our food. I slumped in the chair, opened my padfolio, and pulled out a copy of my résumé. I looked at the piece of paper that told the story of a college experience that was unlike what I had anticipated, and that I was determined to get back on track.

The résumé did not divulge my missteps, but it reminded me of them. Of my first semester and its terrifying professors, failed tests, and wardrobe gaffes. Of my second semester, when my father had insisted I take a second math course, certain that my grade in the first was a fluke—an unfortunate professor, my "adjustment" issues—until another failed test and tearful phone call convinced him that it was time to drop the new class and, with it, his idea of mathematics as my major or, at the very least, my minor.

Since those initial stumbles, my grades had continued climbing, and so had my confidence, until my meeting with Emma brought another slap in the face.

"Breakfast time!" Alex said, as I watched a tray full of breakfast goodies slide onto the table.

When I had first met Alex, his attentions captivated me with a feeling that had escaped me since arriving at Duke—the feeling of being wanted. Being chased instead of chasing. And so Alex, with an overpowering confidence and outgoing nature that I envied, became not just the first boyfriend of college life but my introduction to it: my first time having sex; my first time attending the parties I had originally shied away from; my first time drinking at these parties, taking shots, getting drunk, and throwing it all up at the end of the night; my first time conforming to the culture around me.

"Let's see the résumé that's going to stop employers in their tracks!" Alex reached across the table to pluck the paper out of my hands. Frantically, I yanked it away.

"Oh, I see how it is," he said with a laugh. I forced a smile, grateful that he had interpreted my panicked reaction as playful. "So you'll pass that thing around to strangers today as if it were candy during trick-or-treating, but you won't even let your boyfriend see it?"

Exactly, I wanted to say, but this would be rude. In fact, what I *really* wanted to say was that yes, of course my boyfriend could see my résumé. He did, after all, already know everything that was on it. And yet showing it and discussing it required a level of pride I did not yet have for a piece of paper that, to me, was a reflection of my academic shortcomings.

"That's right," I said teasingly, trying to maintain the charade that masked my anxiety as lighthearted fun, "it's for their eyes only."

But then Alex stood up and stepped toward my chair. He towered over me with the huge smile that had won me over months before. He had a presence about him, a self-assurance that qualified as egotism, but for now it was such a refreshing contrast to my insecurities that I hoped some of his confidence could rub off on me. He planted a kiss on my cheek and simultaneously reached for my résumé. But I was one step ahead of him. In a sweeping move, I placed the document in my padfolio, slammed down the cover, and rested my arms atop it.

"You can't see it," I blurted out.

Stunned, Alex returned to his seat. Our breakfast fell into an uncomfortable silence.

I looked down, thinking of a résumé that was good, but not good enough. And I was afraid of what that meant on a day when I would watch peers just one year ahead of me—and a significant number who belonged to my class—pass out résumés that would make employers swoon. In a year, it would be my turn.

And so the career fair was, above all, a call to action. A kick in the pants of epic scale. On this frigid winter morning, it was a reminder that, in Duke's type-A bubble, the long-anticipated summer vacation is not synonymous with fun and relaxation; instead, it is a three-month-long résumé-building exercise.

Regardless of one's major, a meaningful summertime experience is not an exclamation point on a résumé but a prerequisite. A top job offer or acceptance to an elite graduate program is the prestigious opportunity that sits on the summit. The steps leading there include must-haves like a high GPA, a strong extracurricular record, and summer experiences. If a student spends her vacation lifeguarding at the community pool, she will fall behind and have a tough time catching up. A student columnist for the *Duke Chronicle* best summed up the expectations:

> If you're a Duke student, chances are that you've done your best to pack your summer full of engaging and instructive experiences. If you snagged an internship at a company at the top of the Fortune 500 list, found yourself on track to cure two types of cancer by the end of July, or plan to jettison across the ocean to redesign the socioeconomic structure of a small Caribbean island, then congrats: you're normal. . . . If life's a race, then volleyball on the beach is an unnecessary pit stop for anyone who intends to win it.

A student's first two summers are the hardest to transform into résumé gold. Aside from a small number of highly competitive finance internships, few opportunities are advertised on campus for freshmen and sophomores, and those that exist are usually unpaid. But for the students who arrived at Duke on the coattails of the best résumé and test scores money could buy, this is not a problem. Once again, parents are prepared to pull out the checkbook to help their child achieve a college student's equivalent of the golden ticket. Duke's many well-connected and well-off families often place a few phone calls and/or subsidize living expenses for an unpaid internship in a city like Washington, D.C., or New York. A vast network and several thousand dollars in summer allowance can go a long way toward building that perfect résumé.

An entire business model has developed to feed the near-neurotic obsession with that crucial internship experience. As the *Wall Street Journal* reported in 2009:

> A growing number of anxious parents are pitching in to help—by buying their kids a foot in the door. Some are paying for-profit companies to place their college students in internships that are mostly unpaid. Others are hiring marketing consultants to create direct-mail campaigns promoting their children's workplace potential. Still other parents are buying internships outright in online charity auctions.

The cost for one of these internship placement programs can reach $11,000 for eight weeks. Although freshmen and sophomores may depend most heavily on family connections and money, the playing field eventually evens out. During junior year, we do not find the internships anymore—now, they find us. Money and connections carry minimal weight when a good résumé and strong interview skills are the units of comparison. It *would* be a beautifully meritocratic process if only the experiences that make for impressive résumés and lively interviews had been achieved by meritocratic means. And so on today's campuses, money has become not just a measure of success but a means for achieving it.

"I thought you had it edited," Alex said, and I looked up, grateful that he had broken the silence but disappointed that he had not changed the subject.

"Edited?"

"Your parents proofread your résumé. That's what you said."

"Yeah, they did. Over the weekend." My family had developed a financial divide of our own. My mom, who had been supportive of my decision to attend Duke but vocal about the sacrifices imposed by the tuition bills, encouraged me to follow a career path that would free me from the financial strains she resented. My dad, whose university salary had been sufficient until his two daughters enrolled in private colleges, perceived any grumblings about the financial realities my sister and I faced as an affront to his bread-winning abilities.

In any other decade, my parents' savings would have been enough to send us to college without unreasonable sacrifice for them or any debt for us. Instead, tuition had risen faster than inflation year after year, and by the time I graduated, the cost of a degree from either a public or a private college—after adjusting for inflation—would be about double what it was when I was born. My dad, however, was just fine pretending that this was not so. He encouraged us to find a meaningful career and pursue what made us happy—as he had done—but his lofty guidance was offset by Mom's dose of reality: *Once you graduate*, she told my sister and me, *you're on your own. We can't afford to help you anymore.*

"And they thought your résumé looked good, right?" Alex reminded me.

I nodded.

"Then I wouldn't worry so much, babe."

I nodded again.

"Here, have something to eat." He slid half a bagel toward me.

"No, thanks," I said, pushing it away. My stomach grumbled in protest.

"Laura, you really—"

"I would eat it," I rushed to cut him off, "but I'm just nervous."

"I know, but—" he started again. We both knew that my refusal had nothing to do with nerves.

"I'm just nervous," I said, cutting him off. "I'm just nervous about today."

"All right," he said, dropping the subject. For now, at least.

The culture I had conformed to at Duke was a hotbed of stress. B-plus was an unacceptable grade. Summer internships were a must, as was a bursting extracurricular schedule. College became a game to play, a code to crack. Such a strategic mentality is inevitable, even necessary, because in a competitive environment, it takes experience to earn experience. The honing, and subsequent judging, of résumés begins freshman year, building upon itself with each passing year.

My peers responded to the stress in different ways—some healthy, some unhealthy. There were students who turned to concentration-enhancing drugs like Adderall and Ritalin to get through all-nighters. Stress-filled weeks were offset by binge-drinking-filled weekends. Although dating was common, hooking up and its lack of commitment was far more so, and—much unlike my friends back home who had stayed in Alabama for college—few couples discussed something like marriage; careers came first. I reacted to the pressures in a way that was typical among my female classmates. I recognized that while I could not control something like the curve in a class, there were things I *could* control. So I complemented extreme levels of studying with extreme levels of exercise and extreme eating habits (or lack thereof) that surely qualified as an eating disorder. All this despite my size-2 frame.

"You don't have to do this," Alex told me as he took the final bite of the bagel I had refused. I wondered why I had agreed to meet him for breakfast. "You don't have to go to the fair today."

"I know."

"Then why are you going?"

"Alex, I told you what Emma said."

"You're running behind the pack. I know. I get it." And he did get it, which was exactly why he had chosen to remove himself from the pettiness. To anyone who asked about his plans, Alex said he would become an entrepreneur. He and two fraternity brothers had a couple of ideas and were exploring the feasibility of each one with hopes of going all in and launching a company after graduation.

"You have your track," I told him, "and I need mine."

"But why should someone like Emma tell you what track that should be?"

"It's not like that."

"It's not?"

"No. It's, well—" I tried to keep calm. I was not angry at Alex, only at myself for being unable to answer such simple questions.

"It's just—" I stopped. My heart was racing. "Look—what do you expect me to do? Just sit around and wait for my dream career to fall into my lap?"

"Well, what *is* your dream career?"

"I don't know! I was hoping that maybe I'd have some time to figure that out."

I appreciated Alex's frankness, his willingness to ask the tough questions that no one—not Emma or Trevor the career adviser or any of the people in any of the booths at the Bryan Center that morning, or even my parents—would ask. Yet his inquisitiveness agitated me, not just because of my inability to answer coherently but also because of his sense of self-righteousness when we discussed such matters. Alex seemed proud to have quit the game, but I suspected that he had simply grown tired of checking off boxes that made his parents proud. I wondered if this entrepreneurialism was a short-lived act of rebellion, a case of falling for the idea of being a young and gutsy upstart but lacking the discipline to follow through.

"Laura, it's OK that you haven't figured out what you want. But do you really think you'll figure it out here? Today?"

Silence again. I wanted to figure it out here, today, at the Bryan Center. I wanted to so badly, but I knew I would not.

"Probably not," I conceded, "but I don't really have the time to figure it out, do I?"

"So you'll become a banker?"

"I don't know!" I exhaled heavily. "Maybe. Maybe not. But I will try to find something that will give me time to figure out what it is I really want. Something that'll generate income to pay down my loans. Something that won't cost me money I'm not even sure I should be spending. And then I'll figure the rest out."

"OK," he said.

"OK?" I looked down at my lap.

"OK," he said calmly. I found myself beginning to relax. Alex leaned across our small table and kissed me lightly on the forehead.

"Good luck today, sweetheart."

* * *

During recruiting season, I imagine Duke feels much like Iowa before the presidential primary caucuses. Although many candidates launch campaigns, the underdogs struggle to distract attention from the favorites—in this case, the banks and consulting firms. Their troops arrive in waves, a veritable campaign staff trained to stay "on message." And the message is simple: if you want to make the most of your education, you need to work for us. As with any campaign, there are the standard events. The career fair is the opening ceremony, an introduction to all the candidates. For the banks and consulting firms, this is their big unveiling. Their giveaways are the coolest and their employees the most charming.

But this is only the kickoff for a monthlong romp through campus. An "information session" is typically the next event in the sequence. After jostling for attention at the career fair, these employers return to host an event in which the firm and its message take center stage. The low-key (read: low-budget) firms may rent a small classroom, bring in one employee for a presentation, and offer bottled water as a refreshment. But the banks and consulting firms will not squander a chance to shine. They fly upwards of 15 employees—often including a high-ranking individual such as a managing director or partner—to Durham for a spectacle that puts the low-budget recruiters to shame. Our suitors may splurge on a conference room and catering at the posh Washington Duke Inn for the one-hour sales pitch and then host an after-party in which they invite top recruits for dessert and drinks.

Interviews mark a campaign's final on-campus appearance. The night before, employers may host dinner at an upscale local restaurant. On the big day, some forgo the Career Center's interview accommodations for the Washington Duke Inn and a hotel room for each interview and a catered lounge for those waiting. (After the first round of on-campus interviews, many employers fly students to their offices for the final round.)

Aside from these standard events, the banks and consulting firms find plenty more excuses to upstage their competition. The campaigners know that the more people reached, the better the odds. And these firms have the money to reach, and subsequently impress, a startling number of students. Sometimes they send employees to Durham for the day to chat with students in 15-minute intervals at an on-campus coffee shop. Others fly in to host a breakfast, a panel discussion, or an interview-prep workshop. Remarkably, these employers are simultaneously running similar campaigns on other elite campuses.

Each firm is aware of the significant constraints to winning us over—a target audience with little, if any, business and financial background. We have no familiarity with the ins and outs of the industry, no published rankings to go by, and—for many at a liberal arts school like Duke—not even one finance or business class under our belts. We take everything at face value, so the firms put on their best faces. Material decadence becomes a stand-in for more important criteria. A bank that hosts a steak dinner must be a better choice than one that serves finger food, right?

A young consultant at Bain told me that his firm offers monetary bonuses for uncovering a competitor's latest tactic for wooing students—whatever it is, Bain wants to match it. The consulting firm McKinsey brags about its resort in the Alps that serves as a training facility. BCG is just one of the firms that offer to pay for their consultants' MBA degrees (often a $100,000 tab). Bain boasts about its externship program, in which it grants employees funding and six months' leave to have a go at the job of their dreams—supporting a health-care organization in Uganda, helping a charter school to get on its feet, or maybe working at ESPN. It is a move that cleverly stifles the employees' guilt over choosing consulting instead of the jobs they had always imagined holding.

And then, of course, there are the salaries. Banking and consulting interns are paid about $34 per hour, or $13,000 for just 10 weeks of work, plus a signing bonus or "living stipend" of a couple of thousand dollars. And at some i-banks, interns receive overtime pay. An intern who works 80-hour weeks (as is often the case) and receives time-and-a-half for the overtime work can earn over $30,000 in just one summer; and that is not counting the additional $10,000 bonus she will receive for signing a full-time offer at the end of her stint. Walking away at summer's end with $40,000 may be unusual, but such best-case scenarios can instantly become on-campus legends that students are determined to repeat. These internships are in a league of their own when compared with popular summer alternatives in which most interns earn no salary while the lucky ones earn a stipend of a couple of thousand dollars—neither of which is sufficient to cover living costs in cities like New York or Washington,

D.C., where most opportunities are found.

The aggressive courting of recruits suggests that students who are awash with job offers can draw employers into a bidding war. The basic economic law of supply and demand would predict such extravagance only when the number of jobs dwarfed the number of students. An employer would then spare no expense to ensure that *its* offer was the one accepted. If it were the other way around—if there were far more candidates than job opportunities—salaries would be deflated, just as they are for the insanely competitive entry-level jobs in fields like advertising, fashion, and PR, where the starting salaries do not even cover the cost of living in New York City.

But economic law does not apply to finance. The supply of qualified students vastly exceeds the demand for talent, yet bonuses and salaries are off the charts. The result is a two-way rat race. Students fall over themselves to impress a limited number of banks, and the banks spend recklessly to impress a bottomless pit of suitable students.

Any student who makes an honest effort to sample the assortment of career opportunities will likely find that playing the recruiting game is not too different from flying in the first-class cabin: once you are spoiled by the luxury, it is difficult to imagine going behind that curtain and ever again sitting in the cramped, pedestrian conditions of coach.

And the career fair is where this all begins.

* * *

There was a long line in front of the first booth I visited. A young, attractive woman stood behind the table, wearing a navy suit with a pink blouse. Pinned to her lapel was a name tag that read *Lindsay* and a blue ribbon with the word *ALUM* printed in gold. Lindsay had nice cheekbones, and her hair was pinned back in a way that perfectly balanced the feminine and the professional. She was petite—5-foot-3 and 110 pounds at most—and her suit was surely a size 0. But this is not how any of the students in the Bryan Center would remember her. Instead, the way Lindsay held herself, the confidence in her voice, and, most important, the name on the table she stood behind—Lehman Brothers—added inches and years to her appearance.

I nervously joined the line, not knowing what I would do at the front but thankful for the time to figure it out. I observed a methodical rotation. Lindsay spoke with three people at once, and when one of the students decided to step out, he exchanged his résumé for Lindsay's business card. Then, the two shook hands. The next person in line filled the void, thrust her hand in front of Lindsay's, and introduced herself. The conversation picked up where it left off until another person decided to rotate out.

Not all of the booths churned through students, handshakes, business cards, and résumés like a well-oiled machine. There were nonprofit employers at the fair, too, represented by recruiters who looked bewildered by the hundreds of students who walked by without showing interest. They rearranged their pamphlets while stealing envious glances at the high-gloss booklets on their neighbors' tables. These low-budget firms' one-size-fits-all brochures paled in comparison with some companies' libraries: a brochure just about opportunities for women, another for minorities, one highlighting social-responsibility efforts, a guide to the interview process, and so on. The nonprofit representatives fiddled with their branded key chains, wishing they could afford the banks' free Nalgene water bottles or backpacks. They looked at the candy bowl on their own table and the Tootsie Roll Pops and Jolly Ranchers sitting inside, wondering why they had ever thought that candy could compete.[3]

The cycle at the Lehman booth continued until it was finally my turn to engage with Lindsay. I stuck my hand out, as I had watched my predecessors do. "I'm Laura Newland—nice to meet you." Lindsay shook my hand, welcomed me, and then returned to the ongoing conversation.

"What makes Lehman different from the other banks?" the student to my right asked.

"Well, one of the great things about Lehman is that everyone is so supportive. At other banks, it is extremely competitive. Dog-eat-dog, you know? It can get very tense." She flashed a winning smile and continued, "But at Lehman, when you are in the elevator with a coworker, you're going to start up a conversation with that person, even if you've never met him before."

---

3. Duke hosts a separate Nonprofit and Government Career Fair each year, but the poor timing limits effectiveness. The mid-October date implicitly excludes the juniors who won't begin searching for internships until the second semester and the many seniors who, by then, are already entrenched in private-sector recruitment and have likely been seduced by the much-higher salaries on the table. It's too bad that once January rolls round—when juniors begin looking for internships and jobless seniors reconsider their priorities—there is neither a nonprofit/government fair nor sufficient opportunities at the standard career fair.

We all smiled and nodded as she concluded, "That is just part of the Lehman culture."

The student who asked this question exited the group, seemingly pleased with the answer he received, and was replaced by a student who thrust her hand toward Lindsay with such intensity that I took a small step backward to make room for this powerful presence. Then, before offering the opportunity to the circle's veterans to ask the next question, this newcomer dramatically cleared her throat and said, in a steady and confident voice, "Lehman's most recent quarterly report showed that fixed-income trading was one of the biggest drivers of your soft earnings. In light of this, I am wondering about the types of changes you are looking to make to your fixed-income strategy going forward."

She finished without one pause or stutter. I wondered how many times she had rehearsed.

"Tell me your name again?" Lindsay asked.

"Megan Schmidt," she announced, trying to withhold a smile because a Lehman banker had taken note of her name.

"Come on!" Lindsay retorted, silencing an audience as shocked by the boorish response as by the booming voice that emerged from this petite woman. "You don't honestly care about that, do you?"

For a moment, the heads ceased to nod as we envisioned Megan tracking down Lehman's quarterly report and randomly flipping to a page in search of a question that sounded impressive when, in reality, she likely did not even know what *fixed income* meant.

"I've only been at Lehman for six months," Lindsay added, "and I don't even work with fixed income!"

Behind me, the lined-up students leaned in, eager to hear what had happened and unsure of what to make of this debacle. Some smirked, pleased that Megan's recruiting suicide had just crossed a competitor's name off the list, while others had a look of fear, terrified that one of *their* questions would elicit the same dehumanizing reaction.

Megan had not learned yet that questions should be about one thing: fit. Does the firm's culture *fit* my personality? Do the firm's long-term goals *fit* my professional goals? And on and on. These are not the exact questions that should be asked, but they must fall into one of these feel-good themes. To ask anything else is to shatter the illusion of a process that neatly matches students with employers. Rehearsed and technical questions like Megan's dangerously suggest that employers expect applicants to put on an act rather than be themselves. Likewise, inquiries about numbers—spots available, salary—are off-limits because they imply impersonal priorities. Of course, recruiting is a game that is played and acknowledged by both sides—we compare their salaries as much as their food selection at events; they compare our GPAs as much as our ability to effortlessly become the "banking type"—but to ever admit that there is a game at all is breaking the rules.

Unfortunately, "fit" questions result in formulaic answers that make all candidates feel like a perfect match, but at least they still offer a shot at landing the job. The same cannot be said about Megan's.

"So who's got the next question?" Lindsay asked—her smile wide as ever, her voice chipper and welcoming—as if nothing had happened.

"I—I'm only a sophomore," I stammered. "Are there any opportunities for someone like me?"

"It's so great that you're coming to the career fair as a sophomore," Lindsay said warmly, "and while many banks do offer sophomore programs, Lehman's internships are designed for juniors only."

I nodded.

"So, keep at it. You'll have a great shot next time around! I'll be looking for you next year."

I handed Lindsay my résumé, received her business card, and shook her hand. I slid her card into my padfolio and smiled. *You'll have a great shot next time around*, she had told me. *I'll be looking for you next year.*

There would not be a next year. Seven months after Lindsay scoffed at other banks' "tense" environments, the company filed for the largest bankruptcy in the history of the United States. And Lehman wasn't alone. Located directly across from Lehman's booth on the day of the career fair—in a corner of the Bryan Center that, in retrospect, would seem to have been cursed—was the investment bank Bear Stearns, represented by an optimistic albeit ill-fated trader named Josh. Josh was a former Duke football player and took a more laid-back approach to recruiting than Lindsay. He boasted about the "rush" of trading, and when he learned that I was an economics major, he laughed at his failed attempt to pursue that same major, flummoxed by "those damned math classes!" When I spoke with Josh that January, Bear Stearns's stock price spent the month fluctuating between $75 and $90. Two months later, in mid-March, the Federal Reserve bailed out the bank, and J.P. Morgan purchased

Bear Stearns for the fire-sale price of $2 a share.[4] Josh probably lost his job. The juniors who would accept internship offers that February and the seniors who had accepted full-time offers in the fall never made it to the office; but until the seniors found a backup plan, they lived off the bankrupt firm's $10,000 signing bonus. Four of the investment banking institutions—Wachovia, Merrill Lynch, Lehman, and Bear—whose booths boasted some of the longest lines at the January 2008 career fair did not even exist when the January 2009 career fair rolled around. But students were not disillusioned. That year, among the Duke, Harvard, and Penn grads who accepted jobs, finance was still the most popular industry.

* * *

It is the impenetrable grasp of these employers on even the most eclectic students and dogged do-gooders that prompted a *Duke Chronicle* reporter to open her article on the January 2008 career fair in such a pointed manner: "Selling your soul or saving the world? That was the question faced by the approximately 1,000 students who attended Tuesday's Career and Summer Opportunities Fair." And for the 1,000 of us, Duke made it much easier to solve the ultimate dilemma: whether to channel our potential into making money or doing good. For those who viewed the 109 employers in attendance as a sign of how we were meant to use our diplomas, it was clear where this sign pointed.

The 109 employers hardly reflected a melting pot of opportunity. Although the Career Center promised representation from a

---

4. The price was later adjusted to $10 a share.

variety of industries, true diversity lay within one narrow subset of one industry. The field of business was not represented by advertising, consumer products, retail, and media firms but by the two sectors of finance and consulting. Here, the variety was astounding! Within finance, students had their pick of private equity firms, hedge funds, asset management firms, finance research firms, and financial product rating firms. This list does not even include the variety of investment banks—bulge bracket, middle market, and boutique—whose array of hiring departments dwarfed the one or two opportunities that other firms offered. Within the consulting category, students could choose from management, strategy, systems, and boutique firms.

Persuading liberal arts students to pursue such unfamiliar careers is one of these employers' most impressive talents. Although the typical freshman or sophomore may have little desire to emulate the bankers who are routinely demonized in the media, she *does* look up to campus's most high-profile students—members of Duke's popular improv and a cappella groups, the stars of the spring musical, and leaders who regularly make the front page of the student newspaper. Impressionable underclassmen assume that the job offers accepted by these visible and respected students are, by association, respectable too. So the banks do their best to make it easy for leaders to set such an example. When I spoke with a former Duke Student Government president, I learned that John Mack, then-CEO of Morgan Stanley and a Duke alum, had personally offered him an investment banking job. Mack asked for no interviews, no transcript, just a yes or no answer. The Student Government president told me that he was the fourth president in a row to receive this golden offer and only the first to say no.

There is, however, one blatant exception to the success of the finance and consulting industries. One nonprofit option consistently hits the recruiting jackpot. Teach For America (TFA), a two-year program that places recent graduates in the nation's lowest-performing school districts, attracted applications from 18 percent of Harvard's class of 2010. That same year, it was the top employer of graduates of Yale, Dartmouth, Duke, and Georgetown—an oft-cited figure that is significant but misleading. Although more students may work at i-banks, for example, the job offers are distributed among multiple banks, leaving TFA as the number-one *single* employer.

Regardless, the success of a nonprofit employer offering a salary between one-third and one-half of those of the top for-profit firms seems to contradict the idea of my peers' susceptibility to the campaigns of the banks and consulting firms. But, surprisingly, TFA is not much different. Although they make for strange bedfellows, even TFA is a close ally of consultants and Wall Street—how else could it have achieved such success?

With a recruiting battle plan that mirrors the tactical genius of the banks and consulting firms, TFA has found record-breaking success by appealing to students' insecurities. First, TFA establishes itself as elitist—an employer that hires only the most accomplished students from the most prestigious schools. Rigorous application standards and multiple rounds of interviews create this air of selectivity. The second step is desirability—representatives who boast Ivy League pedigrees plaster the campus with advertisements, meet students for coffee day in and day out, and host many recruiting events. Finally, TFA assuages students' fears of embarking on a career that, to so many, reeks of mediocrity. For those with nagging doubts about turning down the banks and consulting firms, the nonprofit overcomes any misgivings by partnering with its competition. J.P. Morgan, Goldman Sachs, and Bain are just a few of the employers that have official partnerships with TFA, promising to recruit directly from the program's "graduates" after their two-year flirtation with altruism. TFA is now officially part of the popular crowd. By hanging out with the cool kids, it has become cool by association.

Like an investment bank that persuades students to drool over 100-hour workweeks, TFA, with its recruiting campaign, has established an air of elitism that transforms one of the most daunting career paths into a race to the top. And while it is encouraging that teaching kindergartners in rural Mississippi or teenagers on Chicago's South Side is a coveted challenge, it is troublesome that a good-hearted program has become yet another elite name to place on a résumé, a strategic "next step," a platform for bragging rights, and, ironically, a gateway into finance and consulting.

* * *

After two hours, I left the Bryan Center with feet aching from high heels and facial muscles overexerted by countless attempts to manipulate a smile. I had collected an impressive stack of business cards, handed over many résumés, and introduced myself to a number of presumably important people. It would seem that my day was a success.

In reality, the career fair is one of the many dog-and-pony shows of recruiting season—an elaborate display that, year after year, meets few, if any, of its purported goals. The employees I met offered answers so formulaic—Supportive culture! Challenging but exciting work! Exposure to senior executives!—that if the banners had been taken down, I would not have known that each table was represented by a different firm. Social pressures and professional obligations also make it difficult for recruiters to convey the truth at an official event, but it is too convenient for students to overlook this reality. A young Duke graduate and successful banker whom I spoke to two years later described the difficulties of returning to campus as a spokesman for his firm: "When you go to a [recruiting event], you are obligated to do what's in the best interest of the company." But it goes beyond that. Pride is on the line, especially when facing students who look up to you: "No one wants to admit they made a bad decision [about accepting the job]. . . . What are you going to tell a student? Are you going to admit defeat?"

Once in my dorm room, I slipped off my shoes. Like the child who returns from a fair with colorful plastic knickknacks collected from winning beanbag tosses and three-legged races, I threw onto my unmade bed a pile of tchotchkes that would eventually find their way into the trashcan. Little did I know that I was squandering a precious eBay opportunity—Merrill Lynch lip balm, Bear Stearns water bottles, and Lehman Brothers spiral notebooks were relics of a bomb just a few ticks away from an earth-shattering explosion.

There was, however, one lasting effect of that day's career fair and the J.P. Morgan information session I would attend the following week at the Washington Duke Inn. Lindsay from Lehman, Josh from Bear Stearns, and the many J.P. Morgan employees struck me in a way I did not expect. I was captivated by the 20-somethings who were just a few years, or even months, removed from college life. They had returned to their alma mater, transformed and triumphant, spokespeople for the firms you read about on the front page of the *Journal*.

I did not know what to make of it. I felt simultaneously powerless and powerful, as insecure about my own abilities as I was hopeful about what Duke could make of someone like me. These recruiting events had paraded in front of me attainable lifestyles that were as intriguing in their wealth as they were disheartening in their homogeneity. And it all left me as disgusted by the idea of selling out as I was enticed by the idea of cashing in.

PART II

YEAR 3, SEMESTER 2

It's a measure of how rapidly our economic order has shifted that nearly a quarter of the 400 wealthiest people in America on this year's Forbes list make their fortunes from financial services, more than three times as many as in the first Forbes 400 in 1982. Many of America's best young minds now invent derivatives, not Disneylands, because that's where the action has been, and still is, two years after the crash. In 2010, our system incentivizes high-stakes gambling . . . rather than the rebooting and rebuilding of America.

—Frank Rich, *The New York Times,*
  December 26, 2010

CHAPTER 5

Because This Summer Cannot Be Like Last Summer

IT WAS THE stuff of reality TV, but no producer could have bottled a formula so flawless. I can almost see the taglines being flashed, one after the other, on TV screens across America. Dramatic music plays in the background as a deep voice-over narrates the recipe for a perfect storm: *What happens when you take 20 ultracompetitive college students . . . place them in a new city . . . make them live and take classes together . . . while competing for a limited number of internships . . . in the worst economy since the Great Depression?*

When I arrived in New York City in January 2009, the world's greatest economy was on life support. The Dow had fallen by more than 60 percent since its peak in October 2007 and had not yet reached its bottom. Of the country's five largest investment banks, only two remained. In just a few months, Wall Street had collapsed, wrecked the economy, and asked the taxpayers to pick up the tab— to the tune of $700 billion. And then, with billions of these bailout funds still in the banks' coffers, "bonus season" rolled around, and penny-pinchers across the country watched bankers take home $18.4 billion in bonuses—the sixth-highest tally on record.

On a cold and gloomy afternoon that was an appropriate welcome to the world's economic ground zero, I joined 20 of my peers in Manhattan to spend the semester studying finance and gaining exposure to the industry. This was part of a program that is the brainchild of Emma, the professor and former Goldman banker who had berated me for my financial ignorance one year earlier. The participants were all Duke students, and together we would take four finance classes taught by Duke faculty members who were also spending their semester in New York. The idea was, supposedly, "financial immersion," and a series of guest lectures, tours of banks, and networking events would contribute to this aim, but there was no internship or work component. Surely, though, a program spearheaded by Emma, the faculty member most committed to Wall Street, would be the perfect springboard into a finance internship. Or so the reasoning went. (When I participated, this semester experience targeted juniors, but according to the program's website, sophomores are now the intended audience. Additionally, Emma has helped establish a second finance immersion program, a six-week experience during the summer, in London.)

Eight months before, when my peers and I applied for this semester in Manhattan, we did not know the Dow would lose so much of its value before our arrival. When we wrote application essays about learning from the industry's top decision makers, we did not expect so many to be out of a job months later. But even if we had known, we may not have cared. An economic meltdown at the hands of those we hoped to emulate could not disillusion us.

So the 20 of us arrived in New York, eager to enter the very industry that had driven our economy into the ground and learn from the "experts" who had their feet on the gas. Our commitment was sadly ironic. It is paradoxical that Wall Street's monumental success in winning the infatuation of top college students is matched only by a knack for arousing the hatred of nearly everyone else. The reasons why Americans were angry at the industry were the reasons why we found it so attractive—huge bonuses even in bad times and the gall to give them immediately after the taxpayers bailed out the banks. Wall Street boasts an egocentric, shortsighted attitude that is steeped in a feeling of entitlement. Fittingly, the same has been said about my generation.

* * *

"Long visit?" the man asked as the elevator emitted loud beeps on its way to the floor where I would spend the next four months. The red duffel bag in my left hand and black suitcase in my right held everything I would need for the semester. Necessities like towels and linens lay neatly folded next to bulky items like a hair dryer, clothes hangers, and my knockoff Ugg boots. The assortment of winter wear with tags still attached was a reflection of my previously sparse winter wardrobe and my family's tightly budgeted and highly practical holiday season—lined gloves, long underwear, and wool socks as gifts.

"Yeah, I guess you could call it a long visit," I told the man. "I'm living here for the next four months."

"Four months?" a woman I took to be his wife replied, taking no pains to conceal her disapproval. The couple exchanged a judgmental look, no doubt wondering what sort of spoiled brat lived in a Manhattan hotel room for *four months*.

When the elevator arrived at the eighth floor, the couple stepped into a scene that was slightly old-fashioned but elegant. The carpet featured thick bands of red and gold that dramatically swirled together. Opposite the elevator was a painting in a heavy gold frame above an antique armoire. But if the elevator had reached *my* floor first, surely the couple would not have walked out as they did, calculating how much my parents must be paying for a four-month stay. Instead, their smirks would have vanished when the doors parted. Maybe they would have briefly wondered, as I did, if the elevator had traveled horizontally to the run-down building across the street. I was not staring at a painting or an armoire but at a large red vending machine emblazoned with *Coca-Cola* and emitting an obnoxious buzz. The dismal gray paint on the walls was chipping, and the faded blue carpet was in need of a thorough steam cleaning.

I stepped out and looked down the narrow hallway, realizing that this floor looked nothing like the college dorm halls it promised to mimic. There were no bright name tags adorning each door, flyers haphazardly posted on the walls, or bulletin boards bursting with information about concerts, club meetings, and the importance of safe sex. I thought of Duke's familiar dorms and common rooms, where students were arriving and unpacking at that very moment. My boyfriend, Alex, was among them, about to begin his final semester of college without his girlfriend on campus. Alex had supported my decision to go to New York even though, deep down, I wanted him not to. He had recently received a job offer from a small consulting firm and would be starting in the fall. When the economy tanked, he had abandoned his entrepreneurial pursuits—though only temporarily, he insisted.

Why am I doing this? Why am I doing this? Why am I doing this? I asked myself the question that had plagued my thoughts for months, only to repeat, yet again, the mantra whose impact had never diminished: *I am here because this summer cannot be like last summer.*

There was snow on the ground, and I was already thinking about summer. But that was nothing—the upcoming summer had dominated the thoughts and motivated the actions of my peers and me for the past two years. *I am here because this summer cannot be like last summer.*

Students like me who come from families with neither the money nor the connections to generate summertime résumé miracles are woefully unarmed. Luckily, I had managed to scrounge up some worthy opportunities. After my freshman year, I applied to a nationwide fellowship program and received funding for a 10-week internship with a nonprofit in Washington, D.C. It was the summer after my sophomore year, however, that was absurd. I accepted an internship with Congress's Joint Economic Committee, where I worked, unpaid, on Mondays, Wednesdays, and Fridays. To cover my costs, I took on a job at a clothing store and tapped into savings from my school-year job.

I should have just stayed in Alabama. In D.C., I worked nonstop, but instead of holding an $8-per-hour job and saving a couple of thousand dollars, as I would have at home, I worked an $8-an-hour job and ended the summer with an empty bank account. And instead of sleeping in my childhood bed, I slept on a $30 used mattress I had bought on Craigslist that lay on the floor of the small bedroom

I shared with another intern. It was the type of summer experience that made little sense to my parents. They initially questioned the financial toll of my decision but with time grew excited about my chance to work "on the Hill." Whenever they called to ask about my internship, however, I could describe little more than the menial tasks I had been assigned.

Eventually, I stopped trying to justify the experience to my parents. But I never questioned my decision. After just two years at Duke, I had become a strategist, trained to plot my every move. From this perspective, my summer was tactically brilliant. I earned the right to place the Joint Economic Committee on my résumé and discuss the experience (with, of course, some spin on it) in interviews and cover letters. Playing by a new set of rules, no matter how bizarre, had become second nature.

I am here because this summer cannot be like last summer. As I wheeled the duffel bag and suitcase down the narrow halls of my new Manhattan home, I reminded myself that I had worked so hard for *this,* for the opportunity during my junior-year summer to have a real internship that paid a real salary. No more Craigslist mattresses, unstable bank accounts, and $8-an-hour retail jobs where "staying late" meant vacuuming and dusting. Time for signing bonuses, complimentary Yankees tickets, and a job where staying late meant a free dinner and a chauffeured ride home.

I had followed the rules of the game. My GPA sat at 3.695. I was an economics major. My extracurricular record was strong. I had two summer internships under my belt. There was just one thing missing from my résumé: proof of an interest in finance.

"And that's why I'm here," I whispered as I inserted the key into the keyhole and slowly opened my door.

* * *

My roommate's name was Paris and she was beautiful. Although she, too, was a Duke student, we had not crossed paths before. When I opened the door, the first thing I noticed was that her long brown hair managed to shine even in the room's poor lighting. She had pulled it into a ponytail, a casual look that nonetheless accentuated her high cheekbones and large brown eyes. When Paris saw me enter the room, she immediately stood up, her long, thin legs gliding toward me.

I repeated the statement I had rehearsed outside the door so that it would not sound fake. "Hi, you must be Paris. It is so nice to meet you." It still sounded fake.

"Hi Laura! It is so nice to meet you too. Let me help you with your bags. Here, I can move some of my stuff out of the way—I'm so sorry for the clutter." Her voice was powerful and genuine and inflected in just the right spots to smoothly transition from an exciting welcome to a show of concern to a sincere apology. Her smile filled the room, and even in gym shorts and a tank top, Paris exuded confidence.

"Please forgive me for having all my study materials out," she said apologetically, staring at the heap of books and papers piled upon her desk and overflowing onto our floor. She picked up one item at a time, slowly and dramatically examining the front and back of each sheet of paper, before stealing a glance at the doorway, begging me to say something.

When I did not, she added, "I'm sorry, I've just had so much work to do since I arrived." And then, with a stack of study materials in her arms, she turned to me once more with an anticipatory look on her face.

"We don't have an assignment due tomorrow, do we?" I asked, taking the bait. Paris immediately dropped the load onto her desk and looked at me reassuringly with a kind smile.

"Oh, no, no, no," she said. "Don't worry, nothing is due on the first day of class." She casually sat down at her desk, opened a book, and then added, "I've just been studying for my *interview*." And while she awaited my response, she continued to tidy up, as if she had not just shared information even more anxiety inducing than a forgotten assignment.

An interview? I had not expected the *i*-word to come up before I had even put down my bags. I had been looking forward to at least 10 minutes of small talk and comforting tidbits, such as how many siblings Paris had or where she grew up, before something as stressful as an interview was mentioned.

"Oh, an interview!" I said, feigning excitement. On Duke's campus, applications are often due a few weeks into the semester, but my Duke–in–New York peers and I had faced many deadlines well before the semester began. "Congratulations! Who is it with?" I felt the tension in the room rise as I waited for Paris to announce which bank had rejected me before classes had even begun.

She looked up from the book, and when she nonchalantly said, "UBS,"[5] it felt as if the room tilted slightly on its axis, shifting the balance of power to Paris's side.

---

5. The name of the bank has been changed.

"It's been quite rough. The bank just let me know yesterday, and the interview is *tomorrow*. They didn't give me much time to pre-pare." She paused, and then added, "And there is just so much to learn, you know?"

I did not, in fact, know how much there was to learn because I had never been granted an interview; she had likely sensed as much. But I hardly realized the snarkiness of Paris's comment because her eloquence was so captivating. I noticed yet again how effortlessly she was able to control her voice, manipulating a complaint into a call for sympathy that, remarkably, did not sound whiny in the least.

"Oh yeah, that's real awful," I said, surprised that I actually felt a little sorry for her.

Paris returned to her book, and for the first time, I took my mind off interviews and my eyes off the striking brunette who had already stolen the show. I looked around my new room, but there was lit-tle to look at. The walls and carpet were as drab as the hallway's. The room was narrow and evenly split in half, the left side already claimed by Paris. Two beds lay against opposite walls and were loft-ed five feet high to create enough space for the requisite brown dressers nestled beneath. An old, limp mattress with a plastic-y exte-rior sat atop each bed's metal frame. Desks were pushed against the beds' ends, also on opposite walls, so that if each roommate sat at her desk, the backs of the chairs would almost touch. It was smaller than anything I had seen at Duke, and Duke is not known for its luxurious dorm rooms.

I tried to move my luggage into the room, but there was only space for one piece. I left the suitcase in the open doorway, placed my duffel in the limited floor space, and began unpacking.

"That's a nice suit," Paris remarked five minutes later when I pulled out the most expensive item in my suitcase.

"Oh, thank you!" I said, beaming. I admired my suit as I carefully placed it on the hanger, maintaining the jacket's defined shape and the pants' perfect creases. It was professional, well fitted, and a proud possession. And I had not even paid a dime for it.

"Where'd you get it?"

"It's from United Colors of Benetton," I said, running my hands over the fabric to smooth it out. "It's a clothing store, not too different from J. Crew or Banana Republic."

"Yeah, I know what it is."

"Oh, right," I said awkwardly, remembering the day I had walked into the store and asked the woman at the counter to hire me even though I had never heard of Benetton, set foot in a J. Crew, or purchased anything from Banana Republic.

"Last summer," I told Paris, "I interned at the Joint Economic Committee on Capitol Hill. I also got a job at Benetton to earn some money. So, here's the cool part—in July, there was a prize for that month's highest-grossing seller. And I was the winner! With the $250 gift certificate that I received as my prize, I bought this suit!"

I could not help but smile. I had felt such pride in winning, especially because I worked fewer hours than the store's full-time employees yet sold much more. But I had been even prouder of the prize I redeemed.

When I had put on my first-ever Wall Street–ready suit, everything fell into place. Or at least that was how it seemed on a hot and humid day in Washington, D.C., before the markets crashed. As the jacket settled over my shoulders, I had taken a special pleasure in glancing at the design on the lining. This superfluous artistic flair was a heartening reminder of the progress I had made since my (unlined) suit from JCPenney's juniors section. The creased pants were an exciting upgrade from the New York and Company suit whose pants had hung shapelessly on my body and whose cuffs had come unstitched by the third wearing.

"So, what did you do last summer?" I asked, peering out of the closet we shared. Paris smiled at me warmly. I smiled back, assuming that she had enjoyed the story I told and the effort I was making for us to get to know each other. But then she paused for a few seconds, letting my question hang in the air, and I could sense what was coming. I felt the room tilt a little more as the balance of power shifted even farther away from my right side of the room, where I stood, holding the suit I had proudly "won" at my retail job.

"I worked at —." If I had not prepared myself, my mouth would have dropped open when she spoke the name of one of the most prestigious investment banks.

"You interned there?" I asked. "That's where you spent your summer?" As if securing an internship at a top bank is not difficult enough for a junior, it is even more impressive when a sophomore pulls this off.

Before Paris could respond, we both turned our attention to the doorway, where a fellow classmate now stood. The boy was short and well dressed and stepped into our room frantically. He almost tripped over the suitcase that stood in the doorway, and even though he stayed on both feet, I heard a loud *thump* and watched my bag topple to the floor.

"Oh, it's OK, don't—" I started reassuring him, feeling sorry for his awkward grand entrance. But I stopped, noticing that he had no intention of apologizing or even picking up the bag. Something was far more important.

"Paris! Paris!" he cried. "You were right. We are the only ones."

"The only ones," she said in a dramatic whisper. "How do you know?"

"Because I just walked around to all the Duke rooms and asked everyone—" The boy stopped. He turned his head to the right, noticed my presence, and held up his index finger in an *aha!* gesture. He stepped over the suitcase that still lay on the floor, and his other four fingers joined the index as his hand swooped down and dangled directly in front of mine.

"Please allow me to introduce myself. I am Quinn."

"And I—"

"Did you get an interview with UBS?" The words raced out of his mouth.

"Well, no. I mean, I don't think so. I didn't get an e-mail about it."

"Hmm," he said, his lips pursed and eyes cast downward. Then he looked up with a fake smile and added condescendingly, "Well, that's OK. Maybe next time!"

I stood there, dumbstruck. Finding out that Paris had already held a premier internship, that she and Quinn had received interviews with UBS, and that I, apparently, had fallen behind was too much to handle within my first hour in New York.

"You asked everyone in the Duke program?" Paris said. "Quinn, you don't even *know* everyone."

"Well, I introduced myself first. *Then* I asked everyone."

What'd you do next—ask their SAT scores? I wondered.

I was taken aback by the entire situation. As Paris and Quinn continued talking, I found myself staring at the boy, trying to sort through the contradictions. Quinn wore well-fitted and stylish jeans. His light blue button-down was tucked in, and the vest he wore on top tied the outfit together. He was a little pudgy, his face average looking, but his well-dressed and well-groomed appearance made for decent compensation.

Quinn's appearance and the way he had introduced himself suggested a commitment to formality. Yet, everything else about him was buffoonish.

Perhaps it was too early to assign labels, but Quinn reminded me of a type of Duke student I had grown accustomed to encountering—a kid who had spent his adolescence as a geek, only to arrive at Duke and discover that there, his average looks were above average and his nerdiness was acceptable. There was an asymmetry about him, as if he were college's social equivalent of new money.

"Can you believe it, Paris? There are 20 of us, and we got the only two interviews."

I pulled my laptop out of my backpack and powered it up, hoping for a distraction. But when I opened my inbox, I immediately forgot about Quinn, Paris, and UBS. My doubts about coming to New York vanished. I felt the room tilt back toward my side, approaching a balance that made for a more bearable living arrangement.

"I got an interview, too." I had unintentionally spoken these words aloud, so surprised was I by the e-mail that I had just read. My declaration had sounded more like a question than a statement, and my voice had barely risen above a whisper, but Paris and Quinn effortlessly discerned the *i*-word and immediately halted their powwow.

I had brought the room to a standstill. Two sets of skeptical yet captivated eyes fixated on the person they did not expect to earn an invitation to one of Wall Street's most exclusive affairs. I knew that I would hold the floor for just three seconds before Paris frantically checked her e-mail for the same message and Quinn sprinted down the hall to check his. So I made the most of my opportunity. I paused for two seconds, proudly taking control of the tension in the room. And then I announced the best part: "It's with J.P. Morgan."

YEAR 3, SEMESTER 2

What Wall Street figured out is that colleges are producing a large number of very smart, completely confused graduates. Kids who have ample mental horsepower, incredible work ethics and no idea what to do next. So the finance industry takes advantage of that confusion, attracting students who never intended to work in finance but don't have any better ideas about where to go.

—Ezra Klein, "Harvard's Liberal-Arts Failure Is Wall Street's Gain," *Bloomberg*, December 15, 2012

CHAPTER 6

Thirty Minutes to Prove
You Live Up to the Hype

AH, THE FINANCE interview. It is easily the most terrifying part of the recruiting process. When I picked up the nearly 200-page-long *Vault Guide to Finance Interviews*, I learned why stress is such an integral component: "Investment banking and other finance positions are among the most stressful and demanding positions on the planet. Thus, interviews in finance often test an applicant's tolerance for such an environment."

The sensible warning would scare the average person away, and this was exactly why, after reading these words as I studied for my J.P. Morgan interview, I wanted to be a banker even *more*. For top students who avoid "average" at all costs, the more foreboding the warning and the more horrid the horror stories, the more alluring Wall Street becomes. Like a daredevil who cannot turn down any challenge, an overachiever finds her thrill in achieving something that almost no one else can.

The interview is not the only aspect of recruiting season that tests a candidate's tolerance for stress. The entire process is an endurance test, one fraught with rejections, career-changing decisions, and peer-to-peer competition. Our calendars are already bursting, yet there are enough deadlines, networking events, first-round interviews, and final-round overnight trips to warrant a personal secretary. We put our lives on hold to manage the chaos. To-do lists become twice as long and stress levels twice as high. It is a struggle to keep up with schoolwork, and there is little time for sleep. Our futures are on the line. There is a perpetual sense of dread—after going through it all, we face a decent chance of walking away empty-handed.

The fears, tensions, and sleepless nights aggregate, but nothing causes more stress than the social pressure. Until the final-round interviews at a firm's office, recruiting remains at the campus level. Over 250 people apply for just *one* position, fostering competition that is intense and unavoidable. When Wall Streeters and consultants arrive on campus to ferret out the worthy from the unworthy, they unleash a Machiavellian spirit that transforms a tight-knit community into a fiercely competitive jungle.

Recruiting dominates conversations, and rejections often become public knowledge. Having our noses rubbed in our shortcomings is inevitable as friends succeed where we fail. There is also a nasty quirk about the process that brings about even greater duress. Good news—whether about advancing to the next round or receiving an offer—often arrives via phone. Bad news typically arrives via e-mail many days later. Because of this delay, the rejected students often learn of their fate from triumphant peers. There is nothing worse than feeling confident about an interview performance, only to blissfully arrive in class the next day and overhear a classmate brag about the phone call she received.

Pitted against each other, we will do incredible things to set ourselves apart. In January 2010, the professor and former Goldman banker Emma warned the student body that some of our peers were taking the competition one step too far. She submitted a guest column to the student paper and reminded us that résumé honesty falls under the Duke Community Standard. Emma was compelled to do this after catching a student whose résumé misreported his GPA by "more than 0.5."

More than 0.5! A revision of 0.5 is not just a tweak. A 0.5 jump can transform a dead-on-arrival 2.9 GPA to a still-got-a-shot 3.4 GPA. Or, it can catapult that still-got-a-shot 3.4 to a *holy-shit-give-this-guy-an-interview* 3.9. Emma's account was disturbing yet believable. Most employers do not request transcripts, so GPAs are self-reported.

* * *

The most spectacular GPA and résumé, however, mean little once the interview lineup is chosen. After two or three years of building a flawless track record, we have 30 minutes to prove that we live up to the hype. If an interviewer feels let down by the in-person version of the on-paper star, we will not advance past the first round.

With interviews, anxieties reach new levels because we forfeit control. For the first elimination round, expectations are clear: one polished résumé and one polished cover letter. We have the freedom to generate countless drafts and submit our work to multiple editors. Time is not a constraint. And then there is the interview—a limited time frame, no editors, and no self-correcting mechanisms like spell-check to monitor the words spewing from our mouths. We cannot pull out a calculator to find the square root of 3,000, an almanac to find the weight of the Golden Gate Bridge, or a textbook to define "unleveraged beta." An interview occurs in a vacuum—perfectionists have access to none of the resources on which we depend to achieve perfection.

Students who skillfully deciphered the college application process are blindsided by a recruiting process that bears little resemblance to its predecessor. This time around, producing a flawless, one-dimensional portrait of yourself is not enough. Because it is impossible to hide behind a polished piece of paper, many candidates crash and burn in the interview, thwarted by an industry that embraces braininess but shuns nerdiness. Students at the most selective colleges are accustomed to rising to any occasion and always succeeding, only this time, some will not.

Finance interviews are most notorious for something called the Stress Interview. A vulnerable interviewee's most dreaded scenario, the Stress Interview and all its perverse quirks are well illustrated by the real experience of a Duke student named Charlie.

"Hello, I am Charlie Bloomfield. It is so nice to meet you." This is how Charlie introduced himself at his very first interview. The event was held at the Washington Duke Inn, the swanky hotel where I had attended the J.P. Morgan information session as a sophomore. Charlie told me that he had driven to the WaDuke in between classes, been intimidated by the formal surroundings, and entered the interview room a nervous wreck. But things only worsened when Charlie's interviewer, whom we will call Mr. Stern, did not say a word or even acknowledge his guest. Mr. Stern simply grunted. Charlie's introduction awaited a response and his outstretched hand awaited a firm shake, but neither was recognized.

"It is wonderful to be here," Charlie offered as he awkwardly stuffed his unnoticed hand into his pocket. No response. For the first two minutes, interviewer and interviewee sat in their respective chairs, neither moving nor speaking. During the third minute, Mr. Stern began typing on his phone. Finally, during the fourth minute, he addressed his guest.

"What's going on in the subprime market?" Mr. Stern demanded with a curt tone and glaring eyes. Despite the intimidating delivery, however, the question was fair. At that time, the term *subprime* was not part of the public's lexicon—subprime mortgages and their toxic derivatives had not yet wrecked our economy—but anyone who stayed on top of the most basic financial news would be familiar with the mounting scrutiny that these mortgages were attracting. Unfortunately for Charlie, he did not even know the meaning of *subprime*, let alone the goings-on in the subprime market.

Charlie danced around the topic, describing movements in the Dow and the interest rate, speaking generally about the overall state of the "markets," just not the subprime market.

"What the fuck is going on here?" Mr. Stern yelled, his booming voice overpowering the small room.

"Well, in the last month," Charlie beat around the bush some more, "the S&P has—"

"The S&P?!" Mr. Stern banged his fist on the table. "There is shit going down in the subprime market right now. Are you going to tell me about it or not? Stop feeding me this fucking bullshit."

The Washington Duke Inn is not the type of place where people yell and say "fuck." Disturbed by the incongruity and terrified of

Mr. Stern, Charlie sat for what seemed an eternity.

Then, suddenly, he had an idea.

Charlie yelled, cursed—anything to match Mr. Stern's aggression. "Look, I don't know what you want from me, OK? The subprime market is fucking screwed right now. It's so fucked up, all right? Is that good enough, or do you want to keep fucking with me?"

When Charlie told me this, I tried not to laugh. Although we had known each other for a while, I had never heard him curse or even raise his voice. He seemed incapable of aggression. Surely, Mr. Stern must have mocked Charlie for such a pathetic attempt at keeping up with the big boys.

"He loved it!" Charlie told me. "The interviewer was ecstatic. The guy tells me, 'Way to go, man—that's exactly what I'm talking about! You're the first person all day who gets it!'"

Sure enough, Charlie received a phone call that evening. "Hi Charlie, this is Mr. Stern. We would like to invite you back for a final-round interview."

And that is how Charlie mastered the Stress Interview without even knowing what a subprime mortgage was.

Charlie had experienced a common version of the Stress Interview. The interviewer opens with the silent treatment and then shifts to combative mode. In a second iteration, called the Two-vs.-One, two interviewers gang up on one Charlie. They heckle, laugh at his answers, and swap scathing remarks as if he is not there. In either form, the goal of the Stress Interview is to make Charlie believe that he is a piece of shit. The interviewer behaves like a rogue prosecuting attorney, ruthlessly attacking Charlie on the witness stand.

Charlie begins to doubt everything he has prepared. His confidence is shattered. But if he remains poised, Charlie wins the case.

For Charlie, however, winning did not feel so good. After the interview, he searched for articles on the subprime market and learned that subprime mortgages are loans offered to low-income borrowers. At that time, these borrowers were beginning to default in record numbers. Many families were losing their homes.

A public policy studies major who had always planned to attend law school, Charlie began to doubt his attraction to Wall Street: "I wanted to help people over the summer, not be at [name of bank] profiting off the people losing their homes." He considered forfeiting the remaining 15 first-round interviews he had been offered but decided against it. "Some people would kill to have these interviews. Some of my friends were not getting interviews at all." And then, of course, there was the reason why Charlie had considered abandoning his law school plans in the first place: "I was told that students are making six-figure salaries right out of college."

Charlie's next 15 interviews with various banks and consulting firms followed a more traditional format. For his consulting interviews, he mastered the case-study method—a completely separate, but equally challenging, interview format. For his finance interviews, Charlie faced the two standard categories of questions that any candidate is familiar with: behavioral and technical.

"Behavioral," or "fit," questions are the most simple and straightforward. These questions tend to be manageable, although a candidate should never, ever discount the possibility of being thrown a curveball: *If you became the governor of Minnesota today, what would you do?* or *My wife wants me to move to China; convince me.* The first trick to mastering a behavioral interview is nailing a set of questions I like to call the Core Four. No interviewee—not just in finance but in any industry—should even consider walking into an interview without having prepared responses to the following questions:

1. Why Duke (or why *this* school)?
2. Why economics (or why *this* major)?
3. Why finance (or why *this* industry)?
4. Why Goldman Sachs (or why *this* firm)?

The Core Four are predictable, short, and deceptively tough. One misstep, such as admitting that finance is appealing because of the money or realizing at that very moment you don't actually know why you chose that major, will doom an interview just two minutes in. Answers to the Core Four must be seamless and well rehearsed (without sounding rehearsed); they must be concise and include clichés like "I love a challenge" (without sounding clichéd). There is no excuse for fumbling these questions.

Besides the Core Four, behavioral questions include any query that begins with the phrase "Tell me about a time . . ." Here, the possibilities are endless: *a time you led a team and dealt with a team-mate who didn't respect your authority . . . a time you had to give a big presentation, and at the last minute, something went wrong.* Little does it matter that college students have a rather small collection of experiences to draw from—most have never held a job for longer than a summer, and anecdotes from high school days and earlier are ill-advised. When an interviewer asks about a time that such-and-such happened, you'd better have something in mind.

To counteract the behavioral questions and their propensity to incite, and encourage, bullshitting, many a Wall Street interview is interspersed with the more objective "technical" questions. Candidates are quizzed on financial news, banking concepts, "problem solving" skills, and numerical aptitude—anything as straightforward as *What is the difference between a commercial bank and an investment bank?* or as convoluted as *How many square feet of chewing gum do Americans consume in a year?*

* * *

It is likely that all this talk of behavioral fit and technical prowess is irrelevant, and what matters most is something called the Airport Test. With the ability to singlehandedly thwart any student's Wall Street ambitions, the Airport Test supersedes the most polished behavioral answers and the most brilliant mathematical mind. I first learned about the Airport Test when I read the *Vault Guide to Finance Interviews*, which claims that the Test boils down to one simple question: "Could [the interviewer] stand to be stranded in an airport for eight hours with this person?" And if the answer is no? Sorry, game over.

At first glance, this personality screening seems reasonable. A first-year banker spends more hours in the office than he spends sleeping and enjoying leisure time *combined*. It is crucial to "fit in." Besides, interviewers in all sorts of industries knowingly, and sometimes unknowingly, employ the Airport Test to varying degrees. An interview is, after all, a subjective evaluation and not a standardized test.

But there is good reason to believe that the recruiting process for i-banking is unusually subjective. Duke and many other of the banks' "target schools" do not have an undergraduate finance program, so applicants have little familiarity with the industry. Banks say this is irrelevant—they just want smart and driven kids who will learn quickly. But, because the most prestigious banks recruit at only the most prestigious schools, *every* applicant is smart, driven, and a fast learner. Differentiating among applicants becomes even more subjective because banks do not request references, letters of recommendation, transcripts, or standardized test results (such as the SAT, GMAT, or GRE). After the original résumé-and-cover-letter screening process, it all comes down to the interview.

You may be wondering what happened to Charlie. He did not end up working for the firm that gave him the Stress Interview, but despite all that soul-searching, he accepted an internship with another major i-bank. And after those 15 interviews and a summer surrounded by bankers, Charlie had this to say about the Airport Test: "If the interviewer is a male [as is typically the case], he selects the guys he wants to be friends with and the girls he wants to sleep with."

While a Stress Interview tests one's ability to adapt to a banker's rough-and-tumble lifestyle, the Airport Test transforms an interview into a popularity contest, screening candidates for that "wow" factor—smart, articulate, charming, and attractive. In other words, banks are looking for the type of person who can be a jerk one minute and a charming, sweet-talking problem solver the next.

I would soon learn just what this profile looks like.

YEAR 3, SEMESTER 2

||||||||||||||||||||||||||||||||||||||||||||||||||||||||||||||||||||||||||||||||

[Sample question]: What types of activities did you pursue while in college?

[Tips for preparing an answer]: While it may be all good and well to talk about the soup kitchen, remember that you're interviewing for intense, stressful positions. Says one interviewer, "We love to see people who worked part time, went to all six of their classes, earned A's and don't seem to need sleep. Frankly, banks like people in debt who will kill themselves for the big bonus."

> —Vault Guide to Finance Interviews,
>   2008 Edition

CHAPTER 7

The Chosen Ones

I HAD NOT been this nervous in four years. I felt like a high schooler again, reliving the morning of the SAT—the last time I had awakened with knots in my stomach, worst-case scenarios in my mind, and enough adrenaline in my veins to make up for a nearly sleepless night. Then, as a high school junior, and now, as a college junior, I was filled with a mix of fear and excitement over the high-stakes event that could determine my future. The similarities, however, between my high school self and my new, college self ended there. This morning, I did not throw on a sweatshirt and pair of jeans, share breakfast with my parents, and skip out the front door with vocabulary flashcards in hand as Mom and Dad wished me *Good luck, sweetheart!* Things were different now. I was different now. And my parents never would have approved of this morning's routine.

Sure, they would have enjoyed seeing me in the black Benetton suit I had worked so hard to earn. They would have agreed that my pale pink button-down added a touch of femininity and that my black heels completed the look. But their approval would have ended there, because after finalizing the ensemble, I stood in front of the full-length mirror and asked myself a shameful question: *Would a banker want to sleep with me?*

I examined my body from every angle. I found myself admiring how the suit hugged my 5-foot-5, 120-pound frame just tightly enough to show off my figure but just loosely enough to remain professional. When I noticed that my blazer hid any semblance of breasts, I was disappointed. But when I turned 180 degrees, facing away from the mirror and craning my neck to catch a glimpse, I realized that I had something even better to offer. *Find a way to show it off, Laura.* I recorded this mental note: *If the interviewer leads you to the room, walk in front of him—make him stare.*

I noticed how my blond hair shone when it caught the light in just the right way. I grabbed an elastic band from my desk and pulled my hair out of my face and off my shoulders. I liked the up-do—simple, elegant, effortlessly professional. *No, don't do it,* I muttered, reminding myself that the black pantsuit created a sufficiently conservative look. What I needed now was a dash of sexy. And so my hair stayed down.

Would a banker want to sleep with me? Once planted in my mind, the question couldn't escape. So I stood in front of the mirror, feeling dirty, ashamed, but also wonderful—when I looked at the person staring back, I could not help but smile and nod, knowing that the answer was yes.

Indeed, a lot had changed since the morning four years earlier when I had taken the SAT. Then, I had driven 35 minutes down Alabama's back roads to reach the test-taking location in Tuskegee, a nearly all-black town once famous for Booker T. Washington and the Tuskegee Airmen and now infamous for poverty and crime. But today, my car ride was markedly different—the Manhattan skyline passed across my window, a taxi driver sat at the wheel, and J.P. Morgan would pick up the bill.

And this time, I had company.

"Aww, Heath," Paris cooed into her cell phone, "you are just the sweetest thing. If I nail this interview, it's gonna be because of that adorable good-luck note you sent me. How'd I get so lucky? C'mon, tell me, how'd I get soooo lucky?"

As the taxi wound its way through the streets of Manhattan, my roommate, Paris, sat to my left, gushing to her boyfriend. But this did not surprise me—the same love chatter serenaded me to sleep each night.

We had not been in New York for long, but Paris and I had already fallen into a routine. Each weekday morning, we awoke at 7:30, hopped on the subway, and attended class. A few hours later, we returned to the hotel, and on many days, this was when the show began. And what a show it was. Paris stripped down to her bra and panties. She blasted loud music, belted out the words, and occasionally danced around. It was like watching Tom Cruise's famous scene in *Risky Business*, only an interview—and not a weekend of debauchery—was Paris's aphrodisiac.

After 45 minutes, Paris unleashed the grand finale. The girl next door with the ponytail, flat stomach, and polka-dot bra emerged as a workplace hottie. The ends of her brunette hair had been curled into cascading waves. Her face was painted with makeup. She had stepped into a size-2 black suit and slid her feet into four-inch heels. The music still blared, but carefree dancing was replaced by an elegant twirl in front of the full-length mirror as Paris admired the beauty staring back. The transformation was complete.

For most people, interviews evoke nightmares, anxiety attacks, and a persistent sense of dread. But not for Paris. An interview was her chance to shine, and the over-the-top glam session was a pep rally for her walk down the red carpet.

"Which one today?" I always asked as Paris sashayed out the door. I struggled to maintain a blank expression as she cheerfully announced the name of a bank or consulting firm that had rejected my application.

Today, however, was different. On this special Wednesday afternoon, I broke the routine. Once again, Paris got all made up, dressed up, and pumped up for an exclusive Wall Street event, but this time, I was also on the guest list. I had been far too nervous about the interview to carelessly dance around the room and much too self-conscious to prance around in my underwear, but I found myself emulating Paris in one distinct way. After watching her collect offers in abundance, I began to think that she was on to something. So I, too, became acutely aware of my own sex appeal.

Paris was the poster child for the Airport Test. She aced it every time with her brains, wit, and megawatt smile—the quintessential combination for passing the Test in its more benign form. She was easily the most articulate young person I had ever met, male or female. It is often difficult for us women to master our voices, to appear authoritative but not bossy, inquisitive but not whiny, and kind without being a pushover. Paris struck the ideal balance. Her tone always conveyed exactly what she intended, punctuated with perfect inflection, subtle nuance, and a sharp sense of humor. As for the crass version of the Test, Paris had that covered, too. Her large breasts, her long legs, her high cheekbones, and the way she nonchalantly flipped her hair back while discussing the pros and cons of the WACC valuation method made for a different sort of quintessential combination, that of any male Wall Streeter's sexual fantasy. In just 30 minutes, Paris could effortlessly convince an interviewer that she was the person he wanted in the deal room one day, in the airport the next, and in bed each night. And I would soon learn that, if nothing else, Paris delivered on this last promise.

"So, Laura, this is your first interview ever, right?" Quinn asked, swiveling his head around from the cab's front seat.

"Yes," I told Quinn dryly. "Yes, it is."

It was the taxi ride from hell—Paris to my left and Quinn in front. It was a chilly but clear afternoon, just after lunchtime, about two weeks since the evening when I announced that J.P. Morgan wanted to interview *me*. Immediately, Paris had frantically opened her own inbox, letting out a squeal of delight and prompting Quinn to run down the hallway. Five minutes later, he returned to our room and announced, "Laura! Paris! Guess what? We're the only ones."

And we were. J.P. Morgan had chosen us three as the only Duke–in–New Yorkers to interview for a Sales and Trading summer internship. This role, which would place us on the trading floor, sounded exhilarating: hands-on opportunities to research, analyze, and have an impact on daily trading activities. This, at least, was what J.P. Morgan advertised in its published job description. But my wake-up call came, as so many do, when I downloaded the *Vault Career Guide to Sales and Trading*. (This guide, along with the rest of the online Vault "library," is provided to students for free by the Duke Career Center. Many other schools' career centers offer the same service.) Despite J.P. Morgan's promise of a fast-paced summer on the trading floor, the *Vault Guide* warned that, in reality, "the most significant tasks of the summer intern will include fetching coffee and ordering lunch." Although interns in the Investment Banking Division (IBD) may work 100-hour weeks running financial models on Excel until the wee hours of the morning, a trader needs a license to do, well, anything. Making coffee runs, ordering lunch, and shadowing—lots and lots of shadowing—make up the Sales and Trading intern's most important responsibilities. Only on Wall Street is *that* worth $34 an hour.

While "paying your dues" is standard practice across most industries, *paying* dues typically involves some sort of cost. Whether a medical resident, a legal clerk, or an entry-level employee in a high-profile industry like advertising or film production, newcomers in these sought-after careers face low pay, menial tasks, and subservience. But not on Wall Street. Although interns perform tedious tasks and accept an inferior role during work hours, their salary is off the charts, and they spend many evenings attending luxurious social events held in their honor.

When I thought back to my previous summer working double duty as an unpaid intern and a low-paid salesclerk, the position at J.P. Morgan became even more irresistible. To earn $15,000 over 10 weeks, I would have needed to work 188 hours each week at United Colors of Benetton—too bad a week has just 168 hours and the store was open for fewer than half of those hours. Working much less and earning much more sounded good, but it felt so . . . wrong. Much of Wall Street had not yet paid back the hundreds of billions in bailout funds it had accepted from taxpayers, the U.S. economy had shed 2.6 million jobs in the previous year alone, and I was on the brink of earning nearly five times the state of New York's minimum wage for doing nothing more than minimum-wage-type work.

*　*　*

Since that evening when the three of us discovered that we were J.P. Morgan's chosen ones, Paris and Quinn had become an inseparable, albeit platonic, duo. Each evening, they converted our shared room into their clubhouse. I was the little sister, the bothersome tagalong who got stuck listening to "big kid" conversations. With Quinn, Paris recounted each interview question by question, reliving her moments of glory and rehashing every imaginable detail of the only subject she enjoyed discussing. At night, she shifted gears, converting our room into a personal phone booth, her partners seemingly plucked from the *Who's Who in the Duke Finance World* phone tree—alums on Wall Street, professors, Career Center advisers, recruiters. "Your perspective is just too valuable to pass up," she told each one, "and I have a big decision to make with all these offers on the table. Thank you for your advice. Speaking with you has been fantastic!"

And there it was—the word *fantastic.* It was Paris's go-to demonstrative, her trademark. When most people use the word *fantastic,* it sounds over the top, overeager. Few are able to use it in a professional context, but Paris could.

I was trapped. My own room turned toxic, the chatter incessant. I tried leaving, but this was difficult. I had no money with which to explore the city. We had no meal-plan cafeterias where we could escape—even eating was confined to the communal kitchen on our floor. We did not have a campus. Although our classes were held in a New York University classroom, we did not live on campus, have access to most NYU student facilities and services, or take classes with NYU students. (Instead, visiting Duke professors taught us.) My only peers were 20 Duke students, a small and suffocating group that took all the same classes, lived on the same floor, and competed for the same internships.

The stress and anxiety were inescapable. Even when I began leaving the hotel for hours each day, Paris managed to fill the remaining hours with narcissistic banter. From the start, it had been a struggle to fit two people into our small room. With each rejection I faced and each offer Paris received, it felt as if the walls moved in a few inches. It was *her* room—her dressing room, her phone booth, her clubhouse, her situation room. I was a bothersome accessory.

"Man, I'm hungry!" Paris announced, addressing anyone in the taxi who felt like listening, just seconds after she concluded the phone call with her boyfriend. "I wish I had eaten lunch today."

"You didn't have lunch?" Quinn asked from the front seat, never one to ignore Paris.

"No," she answered, clutching her stomach with dramatic flair.

"That's too bad, because I had the best lunch today," Quinn stated proudly, "and I have J.P. Morgan to thank for it."

I looked up, confused by his statement. "Umm, what do you mean?"

"J.P. Morgan paid for my lunch," Quinn said curtly, mimicking the bluntness he had employed earlier that morning when I asked which subway route we would take. "J.P. Morgan will pay for a taxi," he had pompously responded, shocked that I expected to take *public* transportation.

"I'm sorry, I still don't understand," I told Quinn. "Why would J.P. Morgan pay for your lunch?" The interview would last just 30 minutes, and our round-trip travel time was not any longer than that. Complimentary lunch made even less sense than the complimentary cab ride.

Quinn sighed loudly, clearly frustrated about explaining something that, in his opinion, needed no explanation. "Each interviewee is entitled to a $25 lunch stipend on the day of an interview." He spoke like a reporter, briskly and methodically presenting the crucial background information. "This perk is meant for people who come from out of town, but, well, whatever." Quinn waved his hand, dismissing this caveat. "Anyway, this afternoon, I had a powerful craving for Chipotle. It is well known, however, that one person cannot possibly eat $25 worth of fast-food burritos."

Having laid out the key facts, Quinn paused for a moment, letting the suspense build in the taxi before excitedly divulging his juicy story. "So I took my roommate with me!"

"Oh, wow. It must have been a great lunch. I really like Chipotle," I offered, finding our only point of common ground. Just as I had during Paris's lovey-dovey phone call, I kept the snide remarks inside. Pre-interview drama must be avoided at all costs.

"Yeah, Chipotle's the best, isn't it? So—get this—my roommate and I order *tons* of food and head to the cash register, only to find out that our total is $22, including tax. We were $3 under the $25 limit!"

I thought Quinn had finished his story, and I was about to start laughing politely when he resumed, his tone even more animated than before. I realized that his silence had simply been his prelude before unleashing the punch line. "So we ordered extra salsa and extra guacamole!"

I laughed. Quinn beamed, reveling in his shrewdness and skills as a raconteur. He thought my giggles were a sign of a well-told story, when in truth I was envisioning Quinn in the middle of his interview, sitting with a managing director at a mahogany conference table and vomiting the burritos, chips, salsa, and guacamole that he had bought on J.P. Morgan's dime.

"I mean, I know that Paulson wouldn't approve," Quinn added with a giggle, "but that lunch was the highlight of my day."

"Paulson?" Paris asked.

"Yeah, Hank Paulson," Quinn replied, still smiling. "It was only a joke. J.P. Morgan got $25 billion in the government bailout. I think it's kinda funny, don't you? Because J.P. Morgan accepted taxpayer dollars, I doubt that Hank Paulson would approve of the bank spending $25 for my Chipotle lunch." He laughed again.

"Yeah, I know about the bailout, OK?" Paris snapped at Quinn, "but who is this Paulson guy?"

Silence filled the taxi. It was as if the honking had stopped and all the engines on the road had temporarily shut off—or at least that was how it must have seemed to Quinn. I, on the other hand, had seen this coming as soon as he muttered the name Paulson. Just a few days earlier, I had experienced the same shock that Quinn was feeling at this moment. I had learned the secret that he was about to discover.

It had happened on the previous Wednesday. I was sitting at my computer when Paris walked in the door, phone to her ear.

"Oh yes, Sarah, I wholeheartedly agree, which is why I am *so* thrilled to receive this offer. I know the skeptics are worried about solvency, but I have no doubt that restructuring the brokerage division is a fantastic strategic move. The freed-up capital will—"

Paris launched into a complex technical analysis that left me befuddled, though I thought little of it—such conversations were routine in our room. Paris consistently impressed me with financial expertise and an eloquent delivery, proving that she was not just a pretty face but a finance wonk.

Or so I thought. But when Paris hung up the phone on that seemingly typical Wednesday afternoon, everything changed.

"Reading the *New York Times*, I see?" she asked, peering over my shoulder as she often did. "Studying the news for your J.P. Morgan interview?"

"No, I wouldn't call it studying," I told her. "I'm just reading the *Times* for fun."

"For fun?" she asked, eyebrows raised.

"Yeah," I said nonchalantly, "for fun. Why do you ask?"

"Oh, it's not that there's anything wrong with reading the news for fun, but it's just a little, well, weird. I mean, I would never consider the news fun. None of it is all that interesting, ya know? I barely even follow what's going on—and it's interview season!"

As she flipped her hair and laughed, my world turned upside down. I had considered Paris the paragon of an up-and-coming Wall Streeter. I had listened to her boast about a passion for finance, witnessed her nearly perfect interview-to-offer conversion rate despite the terrible economy, and marveled over her prestigious internship as a *sophomore*. Paris had reveled in her role as the Queen of Finance, making me feel like one of her lowly, and ignorant, subjects. Until now. It was empowering to discover that everything was built on a lie.

Now that Quinn was discovering her dirty secret, I wondered whether he would feel freed, or cheated. With both hands, he gripped the armrest separating him from the taxi driver. Pushing firmly, he lifted himself up, twisting his entire upper body around as if he were about to leap into the back seat. It looked as if he was about to say something rude, something to let Paris know how unacceptable this was. I hoped he had the nerve to do it but knew he did not.

As soon as Quinn noticed the stern expression on Paris's face, he looked more terrified than appalled. It was as if he suddenly regretted having the responsibility to inform Paris of her error. He became nervous, afraid that when Paris heard who Henry Paulson was, she would lash out at the messenger. But the question still hung in the air: *Yeah, I know about the bailout, OK? But who is this Paulson guy?*

"H-H-Hank Paulson is—" Quinn stumbled, trying to break the news lightly, "he is, well, Paulson is the Treasury of the secretary." He smiled meekly and then realized his malapropism. "I mean—I mean," he said, rushing to correct himself, "Paulson is the secretary of the Treasury."

And Quinn left it at that. He did not mention that Paulson was perhaps the most influential and well-known secretary of the

Treasury since Alexander Hamilton or that Paulson was the man behind the $700 billion taxpayer bailout of the banks or that, in the last few months, Paulson's name and picture had been on the front of major newspapers, multiple times. Quinn did not say that, given the calamitous and uncertain state of our economy, knowing who Paulson was was not simply a matter of financial knowledge but also a matter of common knowledge.

I would come to learn that Paris taught herself just enough to get by, cherry-picking tidbits about the bank that happened to be interviewing her at the time. With her charisma and oratorical mastery, she brilliantly masked her ignorance, skillfully stringing together a few key facts into convincing and professional analyses.

Our economy was crumbling, and many of Paris's suitors were struggling just to stay in business. I did not know which sickened me more—that Paris did not care, or that her interviewers either did not notice or did not mind.

* * *

J.P. Morgan's headquarters was astounding. I gawked at the 52-story Park Avenue building towering above me, craning my neck until I caught a glimpse of its top. When we entered the lobby, I held back the urge to stop and slowly turn around in a complete circle, examining the exquisite detail adorning the floor, walls, and ceiling. Chills went through my body when the woman at the most impressive front desk I had ever seen checked our photo IDs, called our contact, and placed her hand over the mouthpiece as she announced, "Yes, a representative is awaiting your arrival. The elevator"—she lifted her arm and elegantly directed it behind her—"will carry you to the 37th floor. A representative is awaiting your arrival." When we walked into the elevator, I restrained myself from asking Paris if all the banks' elevators had televisions.

The things I wanted to do and say were off-limits. Paris could not know that the lavish skyscrapers where she had spent her summer were anything out of the ordinary for someone whose hometown did not even have an escalator. Besides, I was not a tourist. The suit on my body, the padfolio in my hand, and the real, live bankers waiting for me on the 37th floor meant that I was an invited guest. J.P. Morgan had sent a signal that this Manhattan high-rise was where I belonged. And although I was hardly convinced, I could not let it show.

When the elevator doors parted, I felt as if I had stepped into the centerfold of a design magazine. I hesitated before entering the scene, afraid that my entrance would disrupt the symmetry. The furniture was refreshingly modern—a bright white sofa comple-mented by colorful pillows, an S-shaped coffee table holding a floral arrangement. Elegant light fixtures hung from the ceilings, filling the room with a cheerful brightness that brought everything, from the ordinary to the extraordinary, to life. The carpet was patternless and the walls white, but even these basic necessities accentuated the space in an understated manner, offering a calming simplicity that tied the masterpiece together.

A thin young woman in high heels, a pencil skirt, and a baby-blue blouse approached us, easily identifying the three young students wearing black suits and holding padfolios. "Hi, thank you so much for coming in to speak with us today. I am—"

"You must be Christie. Hello, I am Paris. It is so wonderful to be here. Thank you very much for having us today." All three of us had stepped forward, yet Paris had subtly squeezed past Quinn and me to be the first to greet the human resources representative who managed recruiting logistics.

How does she do it? Paris's smile was bright, yet there was not a trace of phoniness. Her voice was strong and convincing, a balance of the authoritative and the kind. She placed extra emphasis on frivolous adverbs like *so* and *very* without appearing like a suck-up or a ditz. Her natural charisma, long brown hair, and soft features seized the energy in the room, stealing the spotlight from the artwork and the color scheme. Paris was the focal point.

When Paris stepped down from center stage, I made a feeble attempt to match her effortlessly genuine introduction. "It is wonderful to meet you too, Christie. I am Laura Newland. Thank you for having us." My voice was too high-pitched to sound professional, I could not conceal the fakeness in my smile, and my thank-you sounded as if I was trying too hard. *How does Paris do it?*

"Each of you will be meeting with the same two interviewers," Christie told us after Quinn, too, had offered an introduction that paled in comparison to Paris's. "We have already decided on an order. Quinn, you'll go first, Laura's in the middle, and Paris is the last one. Are there any questions I can answer?"

"What should I do about expense reimbursement?" Quinn said immediately, determined to be compensated for his Chipotle lunch. I tried not to giggle.

"Oh, good question. We'll send you an e-mail with the reimbursement form attached. You can just print it out and mail it to us. Your check will arrive a few weeks later. Any other questions?"

"No, I think we are set," Paris said, answering for the three of us. "Thank you once again for *all* of your help."

"All right, then. Quinn, the interviewers will be out for you in a few minutes. In the meantime, I hope you'll make yourselves comfortable." Christie pointed to the white couch before she left the room. The three of us squeezed onto the sofa, with Paris, of course, sitting in the middle. It always felt as if she was keeping an eye on Quinn and me, afraid that one of us would threaten her dominance.

I pulled my study guide out of my padfolio. I had condensed the most important financial data, interview answers, and valuable tips into a 12-page review packet that I had hoped to read during the taxi ride—a plan derailed by Paris's phone chat, Quinn's lunch story, and Hank Paulson's job description. Since learning about the J.P. Morgan interview, I had pored over the nearly 200-page-long *Vault Guide to Finance Interviews* and the roughly 150-page-long *Vault Career Guide to Sales and Trading*. I taught myself financial concepts that were unlike anything covered in my classes. I practiced brainteasers and calculations so ridiculous that it was almost comical—though I never laughed because I understood the likelihood of facing such a question. I tracked important indices and read the *Journal*. Then, when I finally felt comfortable with the technical questions, I prepared for the behavioral ones. I rehearsed answers to the Core Four and racked my brain for personal anecdotes about teamwork, overcoming challenges, acting ethically, and other interview clichés.

But despite my extensive preparation and the burst of confidence

I had experienced that morning while standing in front of the mirror, I understood the unfortunate circumstances: no matter how good I looked or how good I sounded, I would be compared against a person who looked and sounded much better.

* * *

"H-hello. I'm Laura Newland," I stammered, trying to compensate for my nervous introduction with a big smile. I stood in a rectangular conference room whose back wall was made entirely of glass. The view of Manhattan was breathtaking, but I tried not to stare. Instead, I focused on the two men who were dwarfed by the city skyline and a conference table designed to seat 20.

"Thank you so much for taking the time to meet with me." I held my breath, anxiously waiting to see if either man would respond.

"Hi Laura, I'm David Lieber," said one with a smile. I quietly exhaled, knowing that I had escaped the silent-treatment iteration of the Stress Interview. I now looked at the second man, worrying that harmless David Lieber had been planted as the "good cop" in a common Two-vs.-One version of the Stress Interview.

"It's nice to meet you, Laura. I am Ian Caufield." The second man also shared a warm smile, and I relaxed further, knowing that he had not been assigned the role of "bad cop." My first interview experience, at least, would not be a classic Stress Interview.

David spoke up again. "I'm a Duke alum. And here at J.P. Morgan, I'm a managing director." I instinctively stood up a little straighter, understanding the preeminence of this title and recognizing that if a managing director had taken time out of his day to meet with *me*, I must prove myself worthy of his attention. Luckily, he appeared harmless. He was tall and thin, perhaps 50 years old. He looked modest, slightly nerdy, and fatherly.

And then there was Ian. Ian was so good-looking that it was almost comical. Until this point, I had met many attractive bankers at recruiting events, but now they all seemed merely handsome.

"And I'm a VP," Ian told me, employing the same Australian accent he had used during his introduction. I wondered if this was some sort of cruel joke—was this gorgeous Aussie strategically placed as a distraction?

"Laura," Ian began, "I know you are probably accustomed to a selection process that includes multiple rounds of interviews."

I nodded my head, not mentioning that, as an interview virgin, I was not "accustomed" to any sort of protocol. But I played along, well aware that the Wall Street interview process typically consisted of one or two interviews in the first round and a handful more in the final round.

"We want to let you know that we are holding just one round of interviews for our Sales and Trading internship. This 30-minute discussion we are about to have is all we need to make our decision. We will spend 25 minutes posing questions to you, and we'll leave the remaining time for any questions you may have for us. Do you understand?"

"Yes, I do. Thank you for letting me know," I told Ian, slightly surprised that after all the hours I had committed to studying and after all the money J.P. Morgan had spent to impress students, the selection process would come down to 25 minutes of questions. But I remembered that after describing a Trading intern's frivolous responsibilities as a gofer and tagalong, the *Vault Guide* had added, "The most important part of being a [Trading intern] is to be well liked, or at least not piss anyone off." In other words, a Trading internship—which is, essentially, a prolonged interview for that coveted full-time offer—is a shining moment for the Airport Test. Now it sounded as though my 25-minute evaluation would be no different.

Ian and David took turns asking questions. Some were behavioral—*What is the worst grade you've received at Duke, and do you think you deserved it? If you became a banker, earned all the money you could ever need, and then quit, what career would you pursue?* Others were technical—I calculated a complex multiplication problem in my head and worked on a challenging brainteaser that had a trick answer. And then, at the 20-minute mark, David asked me a predictable question.

"OK, Laura, let's say that your boyfriend has planned an elaborate romantic evening to celebrate your anniversary. But, just as you're leaving the office that day, your boss stops you and says that he has a dinner meeting with George Soros that night, and he wants you to join."

David paused for a moment, making sure I understood the scenario. When I nodded, he asked curtly, "What would you do?"

It was a standard question. In fact, this version was far easier than what is perhaps the most infamous *What would you do?* scenario, in which the interviewee is asked whether she would come in to work when a last-minute problem arose or attend her best friend's wedding.

Surely, Quinn had faced the same question just 30 minutes earlier, and Paris would encounter it just 30 minutes later. And even though I doubted that Paris even knew who George Soros *was*, I knew the answer that both of my competitors would give. I cringed at the thought of echoing Quinn, who boasted about his ethically questionable manipulation of J.P. Morgan's lunchtime reimbursement rules. I shuddered to think of displaying a likeness to Paris, who showed no concern for an ailing economy that was displacing Americans from their jobs and homes and even less concern for the role that Wall Street played in precipitating the debacle.

"I can eat dinner with my boyfriend any night," I told Ian and David, "but how often will I have the opportunity to eat dinner with George Soros? I understand that a job like this will require certain sacrifices but also provide unbelievable opportunities. I am prepared to make those sacrifices and take full advantage of those opportunities."

It was the "right" answer, the Paris-and-Quinn answer. It was the same response that I had performed countless times when practicing similar hypothetical dilemmas.

This time, however, I hesitated before offering my response to Ian and David. But only for a moment.

YEAR 3, SEMESTER 2

The Association of American Medical Colleges estimates that, 15 years from now, with the ranks of insured patients expanding, we will face a shortage of up to 150,000 doctors. . . . The decline in doctors' pay is part of the problem. As we look at Medicare and Medicaid spending cuts, we need to be careful not to drive the best of the next generation away from medicine and into, say, investment banking.

—Karen Sibert, "Don't Quit This Day Job,"
The New York Times, June 11, 2011

Chapter 8

Telling Stories

ACCORDING TO THE bankers' story, Wall Street is a meritocracy, a haven for the best and the brightest and a level playing field where all-American values like smarts and hard work win out. The theme is inclusivity, an idea that grows tiresome but is believable. *Just apply for a position*, they tell us, *and give it a shot. If you have what it takes to make it at Duke, then you have what it takes to make it on Wall Street.* To support these claims, bankers broadcast an appealing list of recruiting dos—*Just be yourself! Just show a sense of intellectual curiosity! Just prove you're up for a challenge!* But students have one weapon to combat these fabrications and reveal a process that is not nearly as meritocratic as Wall Street would like us to believe.

The interview horror story possesses the unrivaled ability to undermine the very story that i-banks pay so much money to tell. The horror story is the inevitable product of the quirks and nuances that make the finance interview so disorienting to its victim and comical to everyone else. When job applicants face stakes that are as high as the rules are subjective, there is an unlimited supply of catastrophic missteps. On campus, tales of humiliated candidates and infuriated interviewers circulate as quickly as the juiciest gossip. We hear of blunders so blatant that they would be catastrophic in any industry and slip-ups so subtle that an outsider could never identify the one misspoken word or misguided action that violated Wall Street's arcane code. The anecdotes are sometimes funny and often alarming, but their appeal extends far beyond cheap laughs or intimidation tactics. Horror stories offset Wall Street's deceitful dos with a daunting list of don'ts.

"Wanna hear about the most disastrous interview performance I've ever witnessed?" This teaser was a typical introduction to a horror story, but I exchanged stunned looks with my classmates because the setting for this telling was as atypical as the person delivering it.

"I think you're gonna enjoy this one," the managing director unabashedly continued as he lowered his fork, dug both elbows into the table, and leaned in toward his rapt audience.

My classmates and I stared at our host, a managing director (MD) and Duke alum, in disbelief. When we accepted his invitation to a catered lunch at the Manhattan office of the large investment bank Barclays, we had expected nothing more than yet another stuffy networking event. Even an unofficial event or informal setting had never before presented an excuse for a banker to veer off message.

"You know," the MD told us, "it's just incredible what some students will say and do!"

We hung on his every word, recognizing that our host's choice of topic was not merely bold but unprecedented. Although we had heard numerous accounts of recruiting flubs, the stories always originated from peers. Now one glance at this banker's snarky smile and childlike giddiness proved that the horror story is as popular among Wall Street's insiders as its outsiders. For us, each misstep adds yet another page to a reference guide of what *not* to do, and for them, each gaffe adds yet another entry to a blooper reel of wannabe bankers' botched attempts at acting as if they belong.

"The story I'm about to tell you," the MD continued, "took place when I had just started at Barclays. So that would be, well, about 25 years ago." We leaned in even more closely, knowing that the faux pas must be a true howler if a Wall Street veteran was still recounting the tale 25 years later.

"So," the MD began, "we bring all the interview candidates to New York for the final round. For lunch, the bank takes everyone to one of the nicest steak restaurants in all of Manhattan. And it's not just the candidates at the lunch. Lots of bankers tag along for the good food. Of course, all the interviewers join as well, many of whom are vice presidents and managing directors. So, there's this kid."

The MD paused for a minute. As he smiled slyly and shook his head, the MD reminded us why the horror story is timeless: though it is nearly impossible to succinctly explain why someone belongs on Wall Street, it is effortless to explain why someone does *not*.

"You see, this kid orders a filet mignon. No biggie, right? But when the server arrives and places the steak in front of him, the son of a bitch picks up his fork and—in front of all the interviewers—he plunges that goddamn fork smack-dab in the middle of the piece of meat. Then, that little fucker lifts the entire filet to his mouth, and with the steak hanging in a delicate balance atop the utensil, he begins chewing off a piece."

The scene was powerful enough to silence us for three seconds as we envisioned a young man eating a filet as if it were cotton candy as he sat in the most expensive restaurant he'd ever been to, wore the nicest suit he'd ever owned, and tried to impress the wealthiest people he'd ever met.

Then, as if on cue, the MD broke into a hearty laugh that eerily resembled a cackle. My classmates immediately joined him.

"Can you believe someone would *do* that?" the MD roared, as if, surrounded by such riches, that "little fucker" would have purposely revealed his rags.

Our host appeared unconcerned that his storytelling shattered the Wall Street illusion that a banker is entrusted to protect. He had admitted what is forbidden but, with just a little digging, is obvious—the truth. With each guffaw that filled the conference room at the ill-mannered candidate's expense, the MD confirmed a process whose playing field is so tilted that anyone without the proper training will tumble to the bottom.

To the MD, the story was hilarious, a reminder of the long line of laughable losers who could only dream of standing in his shoes one day. To my classmates, the story was so outrageous that it could not even function as a cautionary tale of what not to do, so instead it offered an ego boost, reassurance that even though countless banks had deemed us undesirable, there are always applicants who are far more so. And to me, the story was familiar—an honest attempt to climb the ranks, only to be laughed at for not having the pedigree.

"Can you imagine the looks on our faces?" the MD asked.

"No!" a classmate retorted.

"I can't!" another added.

But I could.

I wondered if everyone had stared at the candidate the way those in the mock-trial courtroom had stared at me during my freshman year when I stood there, humiliated, in my JCPenney suit and Payless shoes. Perhaps the young man had cursed his naïveté as I had during my sophomore year when Emma laughed in my face, incredulous over how far I had fallen behind my *Journal*-reading peers.

For these reasons, I never should have laughed. I should have been disgusted by the scene unfolding in front of me.

"So, did the guy get the job?" Quinn shouted from across the table, his goofy grin a fitting complement to the palpable sarcasm.

"What do you *think?*" the MD retorted. "Would *you* have given that fool a job?"

My classmates shook their heads. And as the laughter erupted again, I joined in.

I laughed because I had been laughed at many times, and it was reassuring to be on the other side. I laughed because I was so deflated by my own shortcomings that I was eager to take comfort in someone else's.

"That is just too funny!" I added to the chorus, my sense of right and wrong warped by the rush I felt from a managing director divulging his "war stories" as if we were part of his inner circle.

"I know, isn't it?" the MD replied.

I let out a cruel and hearty chuckle of my own. And it was mostly because, for the first time on this journey, I felt like I belonged.

* * *

When the Barclays managing director regaled my classmates and me with the steak-on-a-stick incident, he set the tone for a recruiting season still in its infancy. His story served as a timely reminder of a process that demands constant self-awareness. Candidates are *always* being judged, and misfits are treated with ridicule, not sympathy. The MD's rousing tale also taught us to roll with the punches. Because it is impossible to predict the whims of an uninhibited industry, those who cannot laugh had better leave.

One day after the managing director shared this valuable lesson, I suffered my first setback. Things began to unfold at 2:30 in the afternoon when Paris and I were stuffed into the small dorm room that we had begun to call home even though I still felt like a visitor. Paris was sitting on her left side of the room, at her desk and hunched over her laptop. I was reading a book atop the bed that sat on my right side of the room, a half whose influence was growing steadily after J.P. Morgan had vouched for my worth by granting me an interview. The scene in our room was rare. Paris was not yakking on her cell or gabbing with Quinn. She was not singing along to the music that often blared from her computer or letting out loud belches, a habit that had emerged as our tenure as roommates progressed. It was a beautiful silence, but I savored my roommate's subdued disposition the way the mother of a hyperactive son cherishes her wild child's occasional moments of calm—with caution.

The trigger was a cell phone. It rang and the room sprang to life. Paris instinctively abandoned her slouch and jolted into an upright posture. I was not immune to the impact of a ringing phone, either, so my head snapped up and my book fell from my hands, even though I was mid-sentence. Then, as had become routine, Paris and I became paralyzed in these upright positions during that split second when the ringing sound permeated the room but the brain could not yet process which phone was producing the noise.

It was an extraordinary reaction to an ordinary occurrence, but this frenzy had become customary in the wake of our J.P. Morgan interviews. Paris and I found ourselves in the part-menacing, part-promising period of time that I like to call the one-week window. The one-week window begins on the day of a final-round interview and ends seven days later. It is governed by an unofficial protocol that goes something like this: if an offer is imminent, it will likely arrive within a week, and it will almost certainly arrive via phone; if a rejection is in store, it *could* arrive within a week and it *could* arrive via phone, but e-mail is probable and the time frame flexible.[6] During the one-week-window, candidates are held hostage by their cell phones because they recognize the unwritten rule that a ringing phone brings news either good or bad, but a silent phone brings only bad. The ring of an incoming call is as eagerly anticipated as the *ding* of an incoming e-mail is dreaded. Unfortunately, both are such frequent occurrences that a one-week-window victim is reduced to a restless, jumpy wreck.

These terms governed Room 1117 from the moment Paris and I returned from our J.P. Morgan interviews. We each understood, but never acknowledged, what was at stake when a ringtone filled the air.

Within a split second, the sing-song music that had interrupted the calm and transfixed our room identified itself as Paris's. I

6. A rejection via a form e-mail is a tasteless snub, especially after a bank pays for an applicant's hotel room, meals, and last-minute flight to Manhattan, then won't even bother with a personal call to deliver the decision.

returned to my book, disappointed by another false alarm and angry for allowing myself to get so worked up again.

"Eeeek!" Paris squealed. "Eeeek!"

I looked up and saw that Paris was not placing the phone to her ear and accepting the call. Instead, she cradled the cell phone in both hands, admiring it.

Although the one-week window is tormenting due to the ubiquity of incoming calls, I knew that this time Paris's hopes had not risen under false pretenses. Undoubtedly, her screen displayed the sight that every candidate wishes for during this notification period—neither *Quinn, Heath, Dad's Office*, nor any other of Paris's frequent contacts was on the other end. Instead, she saw a hopeful sign, an unfamiliar number from the all-too-familiar 212 area code.

"One. Two," Paris counted, passing the time so as not to appear overeager. "Three."

She took a deep, dramatic breath and then answered the call.

Three seconds of silence ensued, and I took a deep breath of my own, anxious about the words about to come out of Paris's mouth.

"Yes, David, it is so wonderful to hear from you!"

David. My heart sank. *David Lieber, our J.P. Morgan interviewer.* That I had seen this coming did not soften the impact.

Paris grinned ear to ear because she understood, as did I, that if a call arrives and a rejection is on its way, an HR representative will likely be the messenger. But if an offer awaits, few banks will squander an opportunity to deliver it with all the grandeur befitting this golden ticket. The process of "selling" an offer, or persuading a student to accept it, goes into motion as soon as the announcement is made. Roles reverse, and the mating game takes on an unnatural form as the scrappy young 20-something without a college diploma suddenly has an investment bank wrapped around her little finger. After subjecting herself to forced networking, irrational interview scenarios, and the telling of countless lies, she wins control. Now it is up to the bank to convince her that it was all worth it and that the imminent boot camp will be worth it, too. Some recruiters host all-expenses-paid office visits—a day full of events designed to persuade the recipients of offers to accept. A boatload of money helps, too, and a phone call and personal appeal from someone like David Lieber, a J.P. Morgan managing director, is a nice touch.

"Ohhh," Paris practically cooed, "that is so kind of you to say. And David, I, too, truly enjoyed speaking with you and Ian on Tuesday. Having the opportunity to learn more about J.P. Morgan and the internship program was just fantastic!"

It was painful to hear the conversation unfold over the next couple of minutes as my roommate received the offer I so badly wanted. Witnessing her subsequent celebration—"*Offer! Offer! Offer!*" she cried in an overdone whisper, announcing the obvious as if she were equally shocked and humbled by something she had previously admitted to expecting—was like watching a superstar try to gain favor by pretending to be the underdog. Then, she immediately began placing calls to broadcast the ("wonderful and surprising!") news.

Paris's behavior would have been more hurtful, but I was preoccupied. From the moment she ended the conversation with David, I was consumed by one hopeful thought: *David is making the offer calls right now. Maybe I'm next. Maybe.* I did not allow my cell phone to leave my sight for the rest of the afternoon. I tried reimmersing myself in the book I had been reading, but concentration was impossible. At times, I stared at my phone, longingly and pathetically, begging it to deliver the same conversation I had witnessed.

When three o'clock rolled around and nothing had awakened my phone from its slumber, I convinced myself that David Lieber must have gotten sidetracked. After all, the markets were still open. When the markets closed at 4, I expected the next hour to be my most promising window of opportunity, but nothing happened. When 5 came and went, I reminded myself that bankers aren't constrained by traditional working hours. And then, as 5:30 approached, the phone rang. My heart skipped a beat and sweat consumed my palms. I picked up the phone and anxiously looked at the screen, knowing the glamorous numbers 212 would be a promising sign of a call from that 52-story building where the elevators had TVs and the offices overlooked Manhattan. Instead, the 334 area code that occupied the screen was an untimely reminder of the Alabama town where I would spend my summer if I proved unable to convince a managing director that he should give me a call. I answered the phone begrudgingly, never so disappointed to hear from my mother.

By 6 that evening, the outlook was grim. When 7 arrived and my phone sat on my bed, lifeless, I knew what it meant. I never expected to find out in this fashion, not with Paris's good news a demoralizing contrast to my ill-fated countdown to 7 p.m. Nor did I expect that after its dogged and flashy pursuit of my peers and me, J.P. Morgan would allow our flirtation to come to such an understated ending—by inflicting the silent treatment upon the candidate it had placed in front of a managing director and 30 minutes away from the internship that famously feeds into the bank's full-time job corps.

J.P. Morgan's indifference to communicating made the notification process more difficult than necessary. With each day that passed, my expectations diminished because I recognized that no news is bad news. But I never gave up entirely. I held out hope for that first week. And for the second week. And for the third. And, then, J.P. Morgan finally got around to sending me a form e-mail to deliver the blow.

* * *

The snub from J.P. Morgan stung, but I quickly rebounded. Soon after David Lieber called Paris, but not me, with the big news, my Wall Street aspirations earned the most authoritative of endorsements. First, Goldman Sachs requested to interview me. Then, a private equity firm asked to do the same. Like opportunities at hedge funds, private equity jobs—even at the entry level—are often reserved for the top graduates of premier business schools or the top performers of elite i-banks' grueling two- or three-year Analyst programs. An offer out of college is perhaps the epitome of the Wall Street dream.[7]

The consulting industry was equally intrigued by my résumé. In an industry defined by an untouchable trifecta—McKinsey, Bain, and BCG—all three firms recruit at Duke, and two of the three offered me an interview.

---

7. Private equity is not consulting, and though it falls under the umbrella of finance, it is not investment banking. Private equity firms use leverage to purchase a company, then restructure it and sell it for a profit.

In the Duke–in–New York program, word spread that I was being courted by the most coveted of each industry. *Where are you heading?* a classmate would ask upon seeing me leave the hotel in my suit. *Why'd you have to leave early yesterday?* another would probe when one of my interviews conflicted with our class schedule. *I'm heading to an interview,* I would reply, purposely omitting further detail in an attempt at modesty. Curiosity, however, always won over as my peers succumbed to the masochistic tendency to demand unnecessary details: *An interview? With whom?* they inquired, knowing the answer would be a reminder of a stinging rejection of their own. During recruiting season, nothing is more comforting than a peer who suffered the same fate, and nothing is more dispiriting than a peer who found success where you found failure.

Oh, um, I'd stammer, *well, the interview is with—,* and when I uttered the pretentious name of a suitor, I observed eyes that grew wide. I detected fake smiles incapable of concealing bitterness. I noticed the way some classmates repeated the name I had just spoken, unconsciously elongating the O in Goldman or the A in Bain.

It was all too familiar. I witnessed the very reactions that had signaled to me, as a freshman, that finance and consulting jobs are what Duke dreams are made of. The inflections in my peers' voices and the expressions on their faces had not changed, but something was different. This time, and for the first time since I had arrived at Duke, awe and envy were directed at *me.*

The impact on me was significant but in a way so understated that it was dangerous. It is not only basic economic law but basic common sense that tells us, that which is desired by the most but attained by the fewest is the most valuable. So with each subtle display of jealousy, with each superlative that a peer ascribed to my success, and with each comment like *Well, I'd just kill for even one of the interviews you have!* I pushed another doubt aside. I unwittingly confused others' attraction to these jobs for my own. All because Wall Street made me feel something I had not felt since high school.

* * *

Early on a Friday morning at the start of February, I took a taxi to Lower Manhattan and entered one of those large and overpowering corporate skyscrapers that intimidated me no longer. A jovial man at the front desk verified my identification and offered directions to a room where a woman from HR shook my hand, recorded my name, and handed me a folder embossed with the words *Goldman Sachs*.

Unlike my J.P. Morgan interview, in which I had feared the worst, with Goldman I anticipated the best. I had added to my arsenal the one defense more valuable than the most thorough reading of *The Vault Guide* and more reliable than the most polished answers to the Core Four. I had found confidence. Never again would I have a repeat performance of my J.P. Morgan interview. At J.P. Morgan, I had allowed my outsider status to haunt me, arousing all sorts of doubts that, surely, my interviewers picked up on. Despite sharp answers, I had revealed in the subtlest of ways that I was not equipped to survive an environment where ego is king and there is neither patience nor time for self-doubt. But those nerves washed away the moment I shook Ian's and David's hands goodbye, thanked them for their time, and processed what had unfolded: in an economy that had brought recruiting to a near standstill, I had earned an interview with one of the world's most selective investment banks. And I did not merely survive, but I excelled. The magnitude of my transformation acquired a new meaning. My untraditional beginnings were not indicative of someone who did not belong, but of someone who *did*. If I had made it this far, there was no reason why I could not make it one step further.

"Find yourself a chair!" Goldman's bubbly HR representative instructed as I surveyed an uncomfortably quiet room that resembled a small lecture hall. Fifteen young men and women were seated, and the stack of folders resting on the registration table suggested that about 10 more would join us. My competitors were visibly nervous. Most sat silently and rigidly in their chairs. They were likely alarmed by the number of students ostensibly in the running for an internship whose screening process—given the economic climate and the small size of this particular department—would be unforgiving, even by Goldman standards.

More students trickled into the waiting room, but the space retained its eerie silence. Some of my peers looked around, gauging the competition by staring at each person for a few seconds too many. Most studied the contents of the folder that the HR representative had handed each of us. Inside mine, I found a schedule of the four interviews I would attend that morning. The first three were one-on-one. For the last one, I would face a three-person panel. Having four Goldman interviews is a daunting test of stamina, and in a sterile room filled with the competition, it is difficult to push aside those worst-case scenarios that haunt thoughts prior to any interview, especially when the unknown lurks behind *six* Goldman bankers. But I was unfazed. The confidence I carried that morning would have been unfamiliar to the outsider who had walked into J.P. Morgan's headquarters weeks before and unthinkable to the teenager who had set foot on Duke's grassy quads two and a half years earlier, never having heard of Goldman Sachs.

The HR representative maintained a watchful eye over the room, as if refusing to believe that a group of college kids could be trusted to maintain such good behavior. I used the time to review the study guide that I had first prepared for my J.P. Morgan interview. Except for the Goldman fact sheet that now occupied page one, the guide had not changed. It remained a stapled collection of papers filled with daunting lists of numbers to remember, terms to spout out, and anecdotes to narrate. The way I treated this resource, however, had changed significantly. My guide had morphed from a lifeline into an accessory.

After my J.P. Morgan interview, I had taken my self-study to the next level, from memorization to comprehension. I knew that immersing myself in all things finance would improve my recruiting chances, and I *hoped* it would spark a passion for the subject. Certainly, I told myself, if I made a genuine attempt to understand the things I was saying and the path I was pursuing, I would appreciate the complexity and importance of the industry. But finance still bored me, and though this was disappointing, I knew it was also irrelevant. All that matters is sounding like you know what you're talking about and acting like you care. It is not expected that either be true. On Wall Street, concepts like passion, purpose, and fulfillment are merely buzzwords that do not enter the equation.

I became very good at faking it, not only when I answered technical questions with a sparkle in my eye for commodity prices or retained earnings, but also when I faced behavioral ones. In the behavioral portion of *any* interview (no matter the industry), a strong candidate does not answer a string of questions; instead, she strings answers together to tell a story. To my interviewers, I told the story of someone with outsider status and insider potential. I recognized that at a school like Duke and a place like Wall Street, my upper-middle-class Alabama upbringing qualified me as "disadvantaged." That such a label could apply to someone so privileged was pathetic, disgusting, and entirely inaccurate. But I would be foolish not to leverage it.

My strategy, however, was risky. If it was poorly executed, I would reveal that I had not fully overcome an unconventional background and, like the steak eater with poor table manners, was not quite ready to play with the big boys. If it was successful, I would prove that my work ethic and resourcefulness trumped inexperience and that I could handle anything thrown my way.

When interviewers asked about my previous summer, I described my juggling act—working at a clothing store to fund my Capitol Hill internship. I never admitted that my internship was meaningless. My interviewers enjoyed it too much when I lauded an experience that was worth the long hours and hard work. When they asked *Why Duke?* I described my high school. It is the only one in Auburn, I would say, and of those who go to college, nearly everyone chooses the university that is just five minutes from the home where

I grew up. Taking an unconventional path was not easy, I assured my interviewers, because my town didn't offer test-prep courses and my guidance counselor didn't even understand the difference between early action and early-decision admission. "I came to Duke," I would close, preparing to unleash my grand finale, "because I didn't want to do what my peers were doing. I did not want to settle for what was easy. I came to Duke because I wanted a challenge."

Oh, how they ate it up! Scowls turned into smiles. Series of follow-up questions indicated genuine interest. These reactions were encouraging, but they were also ironic. If Wall Street's gate-keepers respected leaders, shunned followers, and valued those who took the less-traveled path, my answer would have been swiftly countered with a statement of the obvious: *So why the hell are you trying to go to Wall Street?* I kept waiting for someone to call me out on this contradiction, but no one ever did. By embracing my story, Wall Street was able to adhere to its own.

Goldman Sachs liked my story. So much, in fact, that the foremost investment bank placed me in the running for *two* of its internships, though I had applied for only one. With the first, I advanced through the original series of interviews, survived the final round, and was placed "on hold," or on the waiting list. Citing the dreary economy, Goldman apologized for not extending an offer up front and insisted that it did not want to lose me. So the bank sent me to a first-round interview with a *different* department. I passed this initial test and now awaited final judgment on that Friday morning as I sat in Goldman's holding area.

The last four candidates to arrive strolled in five minutes late and were especially talkative, rambunctious relative to the frigid environment they entered. They seemed unconcerned about their conspicuous behavior and tardiness. I smirked, knowing that such nonchalance could only bode well for the rest of us.

"Thank you for coming this morning," a woman addressed us from the podium as the HR representative looked on. The speaker introduced herself as a vice president, and I listened intently, excited that the morning was finally beginning. The vice president had a stern demeanor and showed little emotion, as if bitter that someone had dragged her away from more important matters to speak to a group of students. Her indifference was in stark contrast to the line-up of happy-go-lucky bankers whom employers typically paraded in front of us.

"It is nice to see all of you here," she continued resentfully, "and I just—" She stopped mid-speech. I looked up, struck by the abrupt silence. I followed her gaze to a person in the front row, a young woman who was part of the late-arriving crew. I suspected that the vice president would direct some of her frustration toward this candidate, perhaps scolding her for disrespecting Goldman's time.

Instead, the banker burst into an unrestrained grin. "Bennett!" she shouted, full of delight, not anger. She abandoned her position behind the podium and approached the person whose presence had captured her attention. She clasped her hands together, producing a loud *clap* that would have caught the attention of anyone who had not picked up on the bizarre scene unfolding at the front of the room.

As the vice president approached, I saw the young woman—

Bennett, apparently—point to her right, where the three other row-dy and tardy students sat. The vice president looked where Bennett pointed and seemed to like what she saw. She clapped once again.

"Michael! Sasha! Collins!" she cried, expressing the same enthu-siasm with which she had identified Bennett. Then, in a move more befitting a baseball player who returns triumphantly to the dugout after hitting a homer than a Goldman vice president with impecca-ble posture and a pantsuit to boot, she made her way along the row with an extended arm and high-fived Bennett, then Michael, then Sasha, and finally Collins.

She disregarded the others in the front row.

"It's great to see you guys back for more for *another* summer!" *Back for more.* The words filled the room as those who had not received high-fives processed what this meant. *Back for more for another summer.* With this statement, the vice president divided the room into two unequal parts. There were the four insiders, the returning interns whose places in the summer's internship class seemed all but guaranteed. And then there was everyone else, those like me who were shocked to discover that in this room of apparent equals, we were the outsiders. With four spots ostensibly claimed in a department of this size and an economy of this condition, we knew what it meant for the rest of us. Of all the recruiting horror stories that kept us up at night, we never imagined that things could go so wrong before an interview even began.

* * *

I dutifully attended my four interviews with little concern for any-thing besides the task in front of me. I pushed thoughts of Bennett,

Michael, Sasha, and Collins aside. With Goldman's bankers, I shared my story with the ease of a raconteur and analyzed the markets with the effortlessness of a CNBC reporter. My back-to-back-to-back-to-back performances went so well that I had forgotten about the "incident" by the time I returned to the waiting room a few hours later.

"Lunch is in the hallway!" the HR representative announced, and I stood up eagerly. The mention of food made me cognizant of a voracious appetite repressed all morning and now set free by a job well done. With a grumbling stomach I recalled the fancy cheese platters, elaborate fruit trays, and hearty sandwiches that lesser banks had served at mere information sessions in an attempt to impress the masses, even though the vast majority of attendants would not even survive the résumé screen. I could only imagine what Goldman would pull off for its final-round recruits. Students scurried into the hallway and I followed suit, but my hopes for a decadent meal were crushed as decisively as my hopes for a decadent internship offer. In a move that neither boded well for a robust hiring budget nor suggested that this bank had any interest in impressing us, Goldman Sachs had ordered *pizza*.

I settled back into my seat a few minutes later, my paper plate, paper towel, bag of potato chips, and pizza slice bringing back memories of kiddie birthday parties.

"Enjoy your pizza," the HR representative encouraged us as the high-fiving vice president joined her at the front of the room, "and as you eat, we will begin calling you, one at a time, to inform you of our final hiring decision."

Greasy pizza slices fell from hands and slopped upon the paper plates. Bewildered stares countered the HR rep's lack of interest.

Each of the 25 applicants had just returned from four interviews and spoken with six bankers. In other words, 150 separate opinions culled from 100 different interviews would need to be aggregated to arrive at this "final hiring decision" that the HR representative referred to so matter-of-factly. I recalled the paper forms that sat in front of each interviewer. My evaluators had diligently written on them throughout each session and then continued scribbling as I left the room. Although it was worrying to see a pen spring into motion in response to something I said, it was comforting to take part in an evaluation that appeared fair and objective. *Was it merely for show?*

"When your name is called, please gather all your things," the woman instructed us. "You will not have the opportunity to return to this room." She turned away from the podium, paused, and then added, "All-righty! Enjoy your pizza!"

My appetite disappeared. I thought of the Airport Test, the subjective screening process that is an accepted, but never acknowledged, aspect of recruiting. Typically, employers at least pretend to mull over the decision for a few days, creating the impression that each person is given careful consideration. But Goldman's rapid turnaround was either an unabashed recognition of the Airport Test or admission of a method even more shameful—the vice president's high-fiving that kicked off the morning suggested that decisions were made before the bankers could cast their judging eyes.

"Dylan!" The first name was called by a woman who poked her

head into the room. A young man in front of me frantically gathered his belongings and headed out, throwing a half-eaten pizza slice in the trash on his way.

"Victoria!" The voice came a couple of minutes later, as if we were patients in a doctor's office, partly hoping our names would be called so that we could get the procedure over with, partly hoping to postpone the discomfort.

"Amanda!"

"Hartford!"

And then, "Laura!"

I forced a smile and shook the woman's hand. Rejections are never easy, but as with the one that arrived from J.P. Morgan, I had been warned.

* * *

There are common fears that pervade every recruiting season. Unqualified applicants agonize over low GPAs, dull extracurricular records, and other woes that thwart a candidacy from the start. Qualified candidates are crippled by more complex concerns. Some are limited by a recruiting repertoire that appeals to only one of the two coveted industries: finance *or* consulting. Others are held back by a résumé that consistently impresses the first gatekeeper but an interview performance that consistently underwhelms the second. And then there is the most menacing concern of any applicant: that she will appeal to both bankers and consultants with a résumé that is impressive and interview skills that are solid—but it will still not be enough.

This was my biggest fear.

When Goldman's bearer of bad news led me into a room not much bigger than a bathroom stall, told me that I was not the right fit, and shepherded me out just 20 seconds later, it should have been a minor setback. Not only had I maintained my place on the waiting list for the other Goldman position I had interviewed for, but it seemed logical to assume that someone on Goldman's waiting list could seal the deal with one of the bank's less selective and less prestigious counterparts. But Goldman's less selective and less prestigious counterparts never gave me that chance.

On Wall Street, there is no method to the madness. During that semester in New York, I developed a relationship with the financial industry that would prove as unstable as the markets. Wall Street sent such disorienting signals that I became part hopeful, part doubtful, and mostly dizzy. The ups were as exhilarating as the downs were crushing, the volatility so overpowering that decision making appeared nothing short of random. An unbearable number of nos streamed into my inbox on a near-daily basis. My application met with outright rejections by virtually every bank and consulting firm that would have been expected to snatch up one of Goldman's waitlisted.

Wall Street's unpredictability is a perfectionist's worst nightmare. I did not know what to do differently or what to fix. Revising my résumé seemed foolish. It had wooed the best of consulting (two of the three top consulting firms) and the best of finance (Goldman, J.P. Morgan, a private equity firm). Adapting my interview style seemed unwise. One of the consultancies chose me as the only Duke–in–New Yorker to advance to its final round; not even Paris could top me. On the finance side, there was no stronger confirmation of my interview skills than Goldman's pursuit of me.

"Maybe," Alex would sometimes offer in an attempt to cheer me up during our nightly phone chats, "none of the other employers are choosing your résumé because they think you're *too good* for them. They do not want to waste their time on someone who will accept a better offer." This reasoning may apply for some candidates, but I was certain that it didn't pertain to someone with a 3.7 GPA, only one major, and no previous internships in the industry.

"Maybe," Alex would try again, "it's just that no one is hiring because of the economy." There was some truth to this statement. In the Duke–in–New York program, offers were scarce for everyone except Paris. But employers distributed first-round interviews with relative abundance, and I watched my peers' résumés receive nods while mine received nos.

"Maybe," Alex would attempt again, but I always cut him off. I had already learned that these were foolish attempts at using reason to soften the blows of a process that is wholly unreasonable.

"Maybe," I sometimes snapped, "you can't decipher it. Maybe it's just arbitrary."

And it sure seemed that way. I was not a shoo-in like Paris, so I stepped in line, took a number, and hoped that my ticket would be called. There I was, on the waitlist for the most desirable employer and shunned by virtually all its lesser peers. My predicament was as nonsensical as a high school senior's being waitlisted by Harvard and rejected by Wake Forest, Boston College, and Lehigh.

This is why a finance or consulting rejection stings more than any other—because it is unlike any no we have heard before. This time, trying a little harder, studying a little more, may not be enough.

YEAR 3, SEMESTER 2

When I taught a journalism course at Princeton a couple of years ago, I was captivated by the bright, curious minds in my class. But when I asked students what they wanted to do, the overwhelming answer was: "Oh, I guess I'll end up in i-banking." It was not that they loved investment banking, or thought their purring brains would be best deployed on Wall Street poring over a balance sheet, it was the money and the fact everyone else was doing it.

—Roger Cohen, *The New York Times*,
September 17, 2008

CHAPTER 9

Do You Not Like to *Drink?*

SOMETIMES, FOLLOWING ALL the rules and checking all the boxes works. Sometimes, it does not. There is a conventional path for getting what's considered to be a conventional job, but when the best intentions fall short, students must adopt Plan B and undertake the daunting task of finding a conventional job in an unconventional way. Without family connections or—in the case of internships—parents willing to pay the way, a last-ditch effort is often doomed from the start. There are always, however, a few frantic job seekers who defy the odds, occasionally because they are savvy and usually because they are lucky. And then there are those who, in a moment of despair, realize that if doing things the right way hasn't worked, maybe it is time to do things the *wrong* way.

Sometimes this works, too.

"Desperate times," Quinn told Paris on a typical afternoon as they engaged in their typical banter, "call for desperate measures."

Although I generally ignored Quinn and Paris's daily chats, or left the room entirely for their duration, today was different. Today, behind a laptop and open textbook that created the guise of careful study, I listened. The afternoon's discussion centered on desperation, a state that Quinn was quickly approaching and a theme that caught my attention because I was right behind him.

It was late February, and neither Quinn nor I had summer plans. The fact that summer was three months away was not encouraging but troubling. The timing exacerbated our predicament because what is perhaps the most ominous and dreaded date of internship recruiting season was just around the corner—March 1. On the first day of March, the unemployed can no longer tell themselves that things will get better and actually believe it. Most postings on the Duke job site have dried up, most slots at the banks and consulting firms have filled up, and what's left are primarily unpaid positions. Those last resorts that have been pushed aside suddenly must be explored.

"It's time to consider other options," Quinn announced to Paris, though neither she nor I had any idea at the time that Quinn's idea of "desperate measures" would be so unorthodox. "The recruiting process has defeated me."

Quinn may have found it difficult to admit his shortcomings to someone who had conquered the recruiting game so effortlessly, but his confession showed no sign of shame or embarrassment. Any disappointment was likely overpowered by the thrill of receiving Paris's undivided attention. On this rare day, it was *his* turn to talk, and with each piece of advice or compliment that Paris threw his way, he beamed.

"I'm not worried about you," she said reassuringly, evoking a predictable and proud grin from Quinn. "You earned that internship last summer when you were only a sophomore, so I have no doubt that you can replicate that success as a junior."

Quinn had spent his previous summer interning with one of the largest and most recognizable global companies, a company I will refer to as Fortune X because of its dominant status on the Fortune 500 list. Under any other circumstance, Paris's reasoning—that one impressive résumé entry should lead to another—would be valid, but the nonchalance with which she spouted this counsel suggested an ignorance of just how difficult the internship market was for everyone except her. She was likely unaware that the already-defunct markets had lost more than 10 percent of their value since our arrival just five weeks earlier and that, despite her collection of offers, *no* offers had been extended to any of the other Duke–in–New York students.

"Right, Quinn?" Paris continued flippantly. "Clearly you have a great résumé and good interview skills, so just do what you did last summer and you'll be fine!"

Though I only watched out of the corner of my eye, it was impossible not to notice how quickly Quinn's demeanor changed when Paris began praising what she assumed to be a honed recruiting skill set.

"W-w-well," Quinn stumbled, his voice flat and his shoulders tight, "I didn't exactly *earn* my internship last summer." He looked down as if he knew that he had done something wrong but smirked as if he was proud of it. "My résumé and interview performance didn't, quite, um, come into play."

I looked up.

Paris appeared as intrigued as I was. "Then how'd you get it?"

Quinn seemed torn, as if he were guarding a secret and wanted to free himself from its burden but was wary of the aftermath. He looked to Paris for guidance, and she flashed the kind and reassuring smile that I no longer trusted, but I knew Quinn would buy the act. And he did.

He closed his eyes for a moment and sighed loudly, then proceeded to lay the groundwork for an outrageous story by sharing its humble beginnings.

Quinn's journey to Fortune X commenced during finals week of the second semester of his sophomore year as he studied in the library late one night. In need of caffeine, he headed to the library's café and stepped into a long line. In front of him stood an acquaintance, who asked the simple question that, from April onward, launches nearly every Duke student's attempt at small talk.

"Whatcha doing this summer?"

"Going home," Quinn answered. "I'm taking organic chemistry at my local university. I'm also working at a science camp for middle-schoolers to earn some money." Quinn was a premed student, and he thought this sounded like a fine summer plan. He smiled, pleased to catch up with this classmate and proud to announce that his plans didn't include blacklisted activities such as waiting tables or lifeguarding.

"What are—" Quinn started to return the question, but his friend was not ready to move on. He disagreed with Quinn's assessment of these plans and voiced his disapproval with just two words that would change the course of Quinn's summer and perhaps his entire career.

"That's *all?*"

When Quinn reached this part of his story as he recounted it to Paris, he shook his head and grimaced, then paused for a few seconds to allow the impact of this retort to sink in.

"I was shocked," he admitted to Paris. "Shocked."

There was another silence, and then Quinn began talking rapidly, the emotions of the exchange still apparent 10 months later. "As this kid told me about his Manhattan internship and big-city apartment, all I could think was that I hadn't even written a résumé! I wanted to jump out of the coffee line, run back to my spot in the library, and postpone all studying until I had something real to do with my summer. Sure, my performance on finals would suffer, but I reasoned that a few subpar grades wouldn't be as unsalvageable as a wasted summer."

It was a story we could relate to. In the coffee line that night, Quinn learned a valuable lesson—that he had fallen behind. For him this lesson was a wake-up call, as it is for many and as it was for me when Emma delivered the news during my sophomore year.

"One week later," Quinn continued his story, "I'm back at home with no internship to speak of. It's the beginning of May and my organic chemistry class doesn't start until the beginning of July. The camp doesn't begin until mid-June. I'm bored out of my mind."

My stomach sank. The prospect of being stuck at home was all too real now that most paid opportunities had passed. But I listened eagerly for this very reason. If Quinn had not found the Fortune X position through ordinary means, such as a relative or family friend, then I anticipated hearing his creative, last-minute strategy for landing such an impressive internship. Maybe I could learn from him.

"So one night," Quinn said bluntly, "I was on this trashy gay chat site."

I stopped pretending to study from that point on. I looked up, eyes wide and fixated on Quinn. I tried to hide my reaction, to not spit out my gum or release an uncharacteristic obscenity.

Fortunately, Paris had it covered. "What the fuck?"

It was a shocking twist to a story that we knew began at a library café and ended at a multinational corporation. We just never expected the middle to be so scandalous.

"And this site was real sketchy," Quinn insisted, in case we were unconvinced. He no longer seemed ashamed by this story. Now he was loving the attention. "You know, like one of those chat sites you only go on if you want to, well . . ." His voice trailed off.

"So I'm chatting with some guy," Quinn continued, "and I tell him that I'm a college student stuck at home for the summer."

"And?" Paris goaded him on.

"And he says that he's a VP at Fortune X."

"And you *believed* him?" I spat out.

Paris's head spun around, and she shot an evil glance in my direction.

"And you believed him?" I repeated, just to piss her off.

"Well," Quinn sighed, unbothered by my inquiry. He had warmed to me in the past weeks, and I could tell that he appreciated an extra member in the audience as much as Paris resented it. "Yeah, I did believe him."

He continued, "So, I write to him, *Oh, Fortune X? Wish you could get me an internship! Lol.*"

Silence.

"I didn't even spell out 'you'!" Quinn added proudly, ensuring that we understood the childishness of what was the closest he came that year to an internship application. Quinn lifted his index finger and repeated the phrase as he drew a large letter *U* in the air, "*Wish U could get me an internship! Lol.*"

Another silence.

"And he said he would."

Days after that online exchange, Quinn packed his bags. Without a contract or official documentation from Fortune X, he hopped on a flight with a ticket that his chat buddy had bought and headed to a hotel room that his chat buddy had booked. It was a ploy destined for *America's Most Wanted*—the sexual predator who lures elite students with the promise of a prestigious internship. But Quinn arrived safely—even had the hotel room all to himself. And the next day, he met his benefactor at the office and started work.

At Fortune X, Quinn avoided the pitfalls of most internships. While interns, *especially* sophomores, are usually unpaid, Quinn earned over $30 an hour—nearly as much as the student who spends his summer on Wall Street. However, unlike the paltry banker who must find summer housing and dip into his salary to cover living expenses, Quinn had no such burdens placed upon him. Fortune X paid for him to live at the Four Seasons hotel. On top of his salary, Quinn received a per diem (a daily stipend) for each day that he worked. And not only did he travel to Europe for a "business trip," but he flew first class.

Quinn spent just six weeks at Fortune X. A short stint by internship standards, yet long enough to earn the résumé entry, pocket a lot of cash, and travel to Europe. He would have worked longer, but there was no time. He had to make it home in time to take organic chemistry.

"I know that I was lucky," Quinn admitted. He recognized that placing his trust in a man he had met in an Internet sex forum was, "well, stupid," he told us. "But I was desperate."

* * *

When Quinn shared his story, I wanted to believe that I was above such recklessness, that my own desperation would never incite decisions so impulsive or actions so dangerous. It was comforting to judge Quinn for his behavior and to question his reasoning with the challenge—*And you believed him?* But Quinn's decision was as understandable as it was shocking. Although the experience said nothing about the recruiters on elite campuses—Fortune X is neither a bank nor a consulting firm and does not recruit at Duke—it exposed much about the premium that has been placed on the summer internship. Two simple words, *That's all?* can induce such feelings of inadequacy that integrity is compromised and common sense trumped.

As a junior without this prerequisite for full-time employment, I was above none of this. A broken economy offers little relief from these pressures, and so I, just like Quinn, could not resist the temptation to bend the rules. Just one week after he revealed his sexually charged internship triumph, I found myself in a situation not too dissimilar, except my unconventional attempt at impressing a recruiter was sparked not by a wake-up call but by the slow and drawn-out realization that after giving my best and coming unbearably close to victory, my best might not be enough.

Recruiting had begun to feel like dating gone wrong. There are the candidates who go through such trouble to appear attractive, and there are the employers that spend lavishly to make each applicant feel wanted. There are first dates and sometimes second dates, fancy dinners and tales of happily ever after. There are promises to call that are met with anxious waiting by the phone. The process is a whirlwind, but the possibilities are plentiful and the opportunities abundant. And, as with dating, everything seems to be going great until, suddenly, it is not. Talk turns from striving to settling, and the most promising pursuers turn out to be the most disappointing duds.

J.P. Morgan was the potential match that shuttled me to a final-round interview but found my roommate more desirable and dumped me via e-mail three weeks later. Soon after, a private equity firm wooed me with an interview and promised to call back the following week but never called. Goldman Sachs sent me to two separate final rounds, teased me with a spot on its waiting list for one of the positions, and promised to call back shortly but never called. One of the elite consultancies spoiled me with a trip to Chicago for a final-round interview and promised to call back within a week but never called. If I had known that I would be stood up each time, these one-week windows would not have dragged on so interminably, with every ring of my cell phone an agonizing letdown.

Inevitably, the snubs and the rejections take their toll. Standards lower, bitterness grows, and the smallest hint of acceptance becomes intoxicating. What was once inconceivable becomes feasible.

For me, it all began because of something called the *case interview*. One of the most formidable tests of recruiting season, the case interview is a defining characteristic of the consulting industry. As if preparing for Wall Street interviews were not burdensome enough, any student who *also* applies to consulting firms—as many do—must prepare for an entirely different evaluation method.

Case interviews sound relatively simple and even a little fun—a business is facing a problem and the interviewee must find a solution. This setup is routine for the undergraduate business students who regularly tackle extended case studies in class but often completely unfamiliar to the liberal arts students who make up the bulk of an elite consultancy's recruiting targets. It is likely for this reason that some firms adopt a practice that can best be described as a buddy system. A student selected for a first-round interview and, therefore, tasked with confronting a case study is assigned a *buddy*—a recent hire and young alum who serves as a resource. This tag-team approach is one of many ways in which consulting firms and, sometimes, i-banks announce their interest and then deploy the troops to reinforce that interest by making each candidate feel like a member of a warm and welcoming community from the get-go.[8]

---

8. Although my first experience with a buddy would prove to be a unique case, I would come to find that a buddy is yet another recruiting perk that sounds exciting and makes the applicant feel important but is ultimately a letdown. Many buddies are unwilling to invest time in the relationship, and despite each one's goading to "ask anything!" few of these consulting newbies have the courage to share any information that a seasoned recruit hasn't already heard in abundance. The relationships quickly turn from promising to burdensome. Recruits often juggle multiple buddies from multiple firms on top of countless other recruiting obligations, and it frequently becomes clear that a buddy consented to the artificial relationship for the same reason the applicant did—as an obligatory networking activity that both are afraid to neglect so as not to insult the firm.

That semester, two of the consulting industry's top three firms offered me an interview. One of these invitations was followed by an introduction from a buddy, a young consultant and Duke alum named Harrison. Harrison and his firm—which I will refer to as Elite3 because it belongs to its industry's undisputed trifecta—were not just another consultant and consultancy that I needed to impress. Harrison and Elite3 represented what was perhaps my last opportunity at landing an elite internship. I would need to do whatever it took to prove myself.

"Let's be honest," my buddy, Harrison, told me after we exchanged the obligatory introductions and shared a few minutes of small talk, "the recruiting process is a pain in the ass."

I laughed. We sat across from each other in a Starbucks on a Saturday afternoon. Unlike the forced phone conversations that thwart many buddy relationships, the rare in-person meeting between Harrison and me was possible because we were each in New York. My buddy was about six feet tall with dirty-blond hair, an athletic build, and a warm smile. He was charismatic and had mastered the most important trait of anyone placed in front of recruits—he was so damned likable.

"I can't imagine," he continued, "how challenging it must be to find an internship in this economy. Tell me—what's it been like for you? How's the search going?"

It is a common, and difficult, question. The temptation to raise your stock by name-dropping is pitted against the instinct to appear available by implying that if an offer arrives, it will not go to waste.

"Well, I've managed to find some success, but the job market is awful. It sure is tough out there." I played it safe, acknowledging my achievements and alluding to my struggles, but never revealing that my "success" had yielded no offers and now I, like so many of my peers, was desperate.

A despondency had set in among the students in the Duke–in–New York program. My classmates were faring no better than I; and, with Paris as the lone exception, most were faring much worse. Our tough luck was especially dispiriting because the consulting firms and, especially, the i-banks were carrying on with their spectacles as if nothing were amiss. They hosted us for information sessions and meals, staging elaborate sales pitches complete with Duke alums as easy to relate to as recent grads and as impressive as managing directors. (At Morgan Stanley, then-CEO John Mack, a Duke alum, even stopped by, gave a brief speech, and answered our questions.) The employers maintained their generosity by passing out interviews as if budgets were fruitful and hiring robust. The juxtaposition of these lavish efforts and the still-withering economy was puzzling, but we embraced the opportunity for optimism. We failed to uncover the Potemkin village that the bankers and consultants had constructed, with each event or interview invitation a misleading display to create the guise of recovering industries eager for interns come summertime.

It was devastating when the inevitable rejections flooded the Duke–in–New York program and employers extended offers to nobody, or only to Paris. The showering of affection and subsequent dismissals left us wondering, as in a dysfunctional relationship, whether it was *our* fault. We became desperate for Wall Street to tell us, *It's not you, it's me.*

"So, Laura," Harrison continued, "if the recruiting process is a pain in the ass, then the case interview is a bitch. When I was in your shoes"—he leaned in and looked to his left and then to his right and whispered—"case interviews scared the living daylights out of me."

I laughed and relaxed a bit because with Harrison, I felt that I was in good hands.

"But I survived," he said, flashing a winning smile, "and I'm here today because with a little coaching, you can knock that sucker out of the park."

"I hope so."

"All right, shall we get started?"

I opened my notebook to a clean page and pulled the cap off my pen and let it hover over the paper. I looked at Harrison and tried to appear more like a journalist eager to hear the scoop and less like a student intimidated by something so unfamiliar. My heart rate quickened, and I assured myself that this was only practice, but the resemblance was too striking to the actual evaluation just one week away. I watched Harrison pull out a folder and nod thoughtfully as he reviewed the material and scribbled something in the margins. For the candidate, these silent seconds are the most painful—you know something is coming, but you do not know what it will be and whether you can handle it. I could only think of the book *Case in Point*, the must-read for case-interview preparation, whose ominous but honest opening is as follows: "The mind is wondrous. It starts working from the second you're born and doesn't stop until you get a case question."[9]

"Your client," Harrison began, "is a—"

The case-study method may be more practical than the traditional banking interview, but it is equally, if not more, stressful. Much of the difficulty lies in a quality that distinguishes these interviews from those in nearly every other industry. With case interviews, the interviewer is not in the driver's seat; instead, he merely introduces a company and its predicament, then settles into the passenger seat and demands that the candidate steer them to the destination. The premise of the case is often vague, the possibilities endless. The applicant begins by taking a right and hits a dead end. She tries a left, but the interviewer, like a driver's-ed instructor, reaches over and grabs the wheel to bring her back on course. Whether she gets hopelessly lost or stays on course until the end could depend on whether she accurately estimates the size of the U.S. energy-drink market or adequately analyzes the dense chart or graph that the interviewer pulls out like a map from the glove compartment. But above all, case-interview mastery depends on her ability to make assumptions, calculations, and decisions—many of them inevitably wrong—while the interviewer glares at her and demands the reasoning behind any assertion.

This is the exercise I practiced with Harrison. We worked through

---

9. *Case in Point* is a gem. Unlike the Vault Guides, it is not part of an established interview-prep brand or series and is not made free to students. It's a book that you hear about via word of mouth. Those who read it speak of it reverently, and those who do not will pore over the *Vault Guide to the Case Interview* and blissfully walk into their interview with no idea that they are—relative to their competitors who read *Case in Point* cover to cover—vastly underprepared.

three case studies—the first about a high-end furniture company whose online business was suffering from declining sales; the second about a big-box retailer that wanted to know the best strategy for entering developing markets; the third about a financial services company that was evaluating the implications of outsourcing some of its operations.

After finishing the final case, I placed my pen and notebook in my bag and stood up.

"You're leaving?" Harrison asked, staring at my extended hand and showing no intention of shaking it. "Why so soon?"

"Oh, I'm sorry," I said, lowering my hand, returning to my seat, and pulling my notebook out of my bag to place it back on the table. I was embarrassed, worried that after a session that had seemed to go well, I had fumbled what I mistook for the ending. "I thought we had finished. I was just—"

"We did finish," Harrison assured me.

"Oh, then—"

"What are your plans for the afternoon?" he asked pointedly.

"I was, um—"

"There's a Duke game that starts in 20 minutes. Let me take you to my favorite sports bar for watching basketball."

It was a surprising offer. I was taken aback by the abrupt transition from the professional to the personal, but it was precisely because of the uncharacteristic nature of the request that I smiled at Harrison and nodded, "Yeah, OK. That sounds like fun. Let's go."

Harrison's invitation presented a rare opportunity, a welcome and auspicious departure from the stuffiness that defines traditional recruiting events. Such an informal get-together could benefit me in two distinct ways, but only if I let it. By playing my hand correctly, I could teach Harrison something about me that neither he nor anyone else at Elite3 would have the opportunity to learn otherwise. Likewise, Harrison could teach me something about Elite3 that neither I nor any of my peers clamoring to impress the firm would have the opportunity to learn otherwise. A casual environment allows an applicant to escape the stresses of recruiting and make a strong case for mastery of the Airport Test. It also allows a consultant like Harrison to escape the demands of maintaining his profession's messianic reputation—the truth is no longer off-limits.

* * *

"Diet Coke?!" Harrison placed both hands on the table and playfully shouted his disbelief as I placed my order. "You need a beer."

"I can't," I admitted as our server walked away. "I'm not 21 yet."

It was a drink selection I would have made regardless of my legal status. Avoiding alcohol in a recruiting setting seemed wise, a common-sense precaution and a rule I had once read in a Career Center pamphlet or something of the sort that included a list like *Top Five Things to NEVER Do If You Want to Land That Job!*

"Oh," Harrison remarked. "So do you have a fake ID?"

That Harrison would ask such a delicate question was as surprising as a tone that implied my answer should be yes. I fidgeted in my chair and unconsciously reached into the purse sitting on my lap, clutching the wallet inside which my older sister's ID was surreptitiously tucked behind my own. I was eager to please Harrison yet convinced that admitting illegal behavior to an Elite3 consultant would reflect poor judgment. As with the no-alcohol rule of thumb, I recalled an insight that many consultants on the recruiting trail had offered, a piece of advice that stuck with me not because I heard it so many times but because, unlike the worthless clichés about working hard and just being yourself, this tidbit seemed valuable — *the way an applicant presents herself to recruiters is the most telling signal of how that applicant will behave in front of a client.*

"Actually," I assured Harrison, certain that his question about the fake ID was a test, "Diet Coke is great!" I smiled, knowing I had passed the test. *Can you imagine,* I envisioned Harrison warning my interviewers if I had fallen for his trap, *what Laura could pull in front of the client if she thought it was acceptable to show me her fake ID? Clearly, this kid has a lot to learn!*

The server delivered our drinks and I took a long, satisfying sip, pleased with my diplomatic answer and proud of the reasoning that steered me away from a regrettable decision. Even though a buddy like Harrison does not, technically, have an official say in the selection process, a student should never assume objectivity. People talk. Especially at a small firm like Elite3.

I looked at Harrison, but he appeared more puzzled than impressed.

"Laura," he pressed, "you can't possibly be happy with a soft drink. We've gotta get you a beer."

"W-w-ell," I stumbled, "give me a month and I'll be able to legally have one!" I tacked on a nervous laugh to hide the fact that I had no idea how to handle the situation, but this seemed only to turn Harrison's confusion into concern. In an attempt to buy time,

I looked at one of the bar's countless TV screens and was reminded why we had come here in the first place. The basketball game was well into the first half, and Duke was winning, but Harrison's eyes rested solely on me. I had thought a sober afternoon watching basketball would strike that perfect balance between embracing the casual and maintaining the professional. Apparently, Harrison had something different in mind.

"Don't tell me," he went on, "that you came to New York for an entire semester and didn't even get a fake ID for going out, partying, and getting trashed?" I clasped my fingers more tightly around the driver's license I had cajoled from my sister yet rarely used because I had no money to spend on—as Harrison put it—going out, partying, and getting trashed.

"Unless," he said ominously, and I could tell that he was entertaining a distressing thought, "do you not like to *drink*?"

It was more of an accusation than a question. The disbelief on Harrison's face and in his voice superseded any inclination of mine to follow the "rules." It was suddenly apparent that professionalism had long been thrown out the window. I tried to suppress a panicked look, terrified that my prudence had sabotaged such a promising opportunity. Harrison was—as I suspected—testing me, but this was a version of the Airport Test that I had not anticipated. I felt foolish for assuming that to ace the Airport Test, a candidate must prove that, in the event of a significant flight delay, she can pass the time with riveting conversation at the airport gate rather than drink away the time with drunken banter at the airport bar. I had a fleeting opportunity to salvage my reputation.

"Are you kidding me?" I rushed to my own defense, placing both hands on the table and leaning in. "What kind of college student doesn't like to drink?"

I triumphantly pulled out my sister's ID. I framed the license with my index finger along its top edge and my thumb on its bottom and let it hover over the middle of the table, right at Harrison's eye level. "Of course I drink! And boy does this help!"

He leaned in, examining the Alabama license and the picture of the blond female whose resemblance to me was remarkable but not perfect, and whose birth year was a legally appropriate 1986.

Harrison's face lit up, and relief overtook mine.

"My older sister," I clarified.

"Sweeeeeet!" Harrison raised his hand above the table, and I met it with a high-five, encouraged by what I assumed to be an act of camaraderie until he let his hand rest against mine for a second too long.

"Let me buy you a beer!" he insisted. I knew there was only one acceptable answer.

"All right," I acquiesced, "a beer sounds great."

"Perfect!" Harrison shouted, flagging the server, who checked and, thankfully, accepted the illegitimate ID offered by my quivering hand.

Harrison's transformation from formal professional to flirtatious partier was as unsettling as my own. Sitting across from an Elite3 consultant and playing the role of drinking buddy, when just an hour ago we had been interview-prep buddies, felt unnatural, a disorienting shift from the strait-laced strategy that had taken me

173

far, but not far enough. Each rejection had bolstered the case for a tactical overhaul; maybe this was exactly the jump-start I needed.

I had not been able to push aside the troubling warning I had heard just one week earlier when the founder of the Duke–in–New York program, Emma, paid a visit. "The Career Center and I were expecting banks to hire half as many interns relative to last year," she told my classmates and me. "In fact, what we're seeing is that they're only taking one-third as many." She shook her head in disbelief. I did not want to ask, but I assumed she meant that *individual* banks were making one-third as many offers. I shuddered to think of the actual fraction of available internships relative to the previous year—certainly a number more dismal than one-third—if she counted the banks that had *no* offers to make because they no longer existed.

"It's brutal out there. Just brutal," Emma repeated. "One-third as many as last year."

It was bad news that, at first, felt so good to hear—quantifiable assurance that my classmates and I were not at fault. The relief, however, was fleeting as bitterness set in—*Why us? Why this year?* This was quickly followed by panic as we grasped the implications of this statistic. An already-competitive process had become three times more competitive. We would have to work three times harder to set ourselves apart.[10]

---

10. It was during that visit of Emma's—and through a few more interactions we would have before my graduation—that I acquired a respect for her that had eluded me during our first, upsetting encounter in my sophomore year. Then, the nuances of Emma's personality had been imperceptible amid the deluge of

"This beer is great." I told Harrison.

"Isn't it?" he beamed. "If you intern with Elite3," he advised, "you better be ready to drink. Man, do we know how to have a good time! Work hard, play hard—you know?"

I was aware of the frat-house mentality that pervades many banks and consulting firms, but I had never heard an employee so openly acknowledge this aspect of the culture.

"It's important," Harrison told me.

"What's important?"

"Drinking and stuff." He shrugged. "You know, being able to have fun."

"Yes, but—" I began, but paused for a minute, debating whether to ask the question that all want to know but few dare to ask. Then I went ahead and asked, "But how can you tell? How do you know if an applicant is fun or not?"

"Let's just say," Harrison said slyly, picking up his beer, taking a sip, and then slowly lowering his glass, "we have our ways."

"Ohhh, I see!" I said with a disbelieving grin. I nodded my head dramatically, feigning comprehension in an attempt to mock the senselessness of his comment. "You have your *ways*!"

---

inopportune advice. Now she provided a refreshing reprieve from the superficiality I had come to accept as the norm on Wall Street. I appreciated Emma's honesty about the dismal recruiting scene, and I was heartened by the sincerity of her efforts to help my classmates and me overcome this. Emma possessed a passion that I had yet to encounter during a semester in Manhattan surrounded by bankers—a passion for finance as a *discipline*. And it was this authentic interest, I would come to believe, that inspired her to create opportunities for her students.

Harrison laughed. I could tell he liked that I was pushing back.

He sat up straight and cleared his throat, acquiring a stern look and playing along with the act. "Yes," he insisted, his authoritative tone undermined by the slightest hint of a smile, "we have our ways."

I sensed that Harrison was eager to entertain me with a story he had no right to share, so I sat silently and patiently. I knew it would not take long for him to give in.

"So we have books of résumés," he announced with a heavy sigh just five seconds later, "one book for each of our target schools."

Clearly loving the spotlight, Harrison went on to describe the exciting day when the Duke résumé book arrived in Elite3's office and the Duke alums gathered around to flip through and choose their favorites—maybe a friend, a fraternity brother, or someone who for whatever reason caught their eye and seemed worthy of an interview. These picks, along with those selected by HR, made up Elite3's pool of first-round interview candidates.

This process, Harrison warned, has its flaws. Résumés say only so much about a person, and inevitably there are disagreements over who earns a coveted interview slot. Fortunately, Harrison assured me, there is a simple remedy.

"That's what Facebook is for!"

As with the warning about avoiding alcohol, I had read and heard much about monitoring my Facebook profile and online identity. *Don't post anything unprofessional that a recruiter could see,* the warning would go, heralded by pamphlets, posters, Career Center advisers, and any member on any of the countless on-campus panels about navigating the recruiting process. *Don't think employers won't look—because they will!*

"Last week, for example," Harrison continued, "we couldn't decide between these two candidates. So we put them through the Facebook test. One of the candidates' profiles," he continued nonchalantly, assuming I knew all about this evaluation method, "included lots of photos of this guy drinking, partying. You know, just having a good time."

"And the other?" I asked, suspecting a clean and professional profile.

Harrison lowered his voice and leaned in. "The other candidate," he said regretfully, "looked boring." I obediently shook my head in dismay. In a way, the advice of the career "experts" was correct. Employers *will* look, but according to Harrison, the fallacy in their argument rested in what, exactly, some employers are looking *for*. I wondered when I would no longer be surprised by a behind-the-scenes reality that was nothing like the wholesome image painted by the flashy campaigns and rigorous selection process.

"So you picked the fun one?"

"Hell, yeah!" Harrison exclaimed.

"Good choice!" I shot back.

The Facebook test was superficial and crude, and in a way it made sense. There is an excess of students able to complete the rudimentary tasks of an entry-level consultant. It is only natural to resort to alternative screening criteria. In the consulting industry especially, little matters more than likability. To a much greater extent than bankers, consultants must thrive in an intensely social environment. Projects tend to be heavily team oriented, and because of the travel-heavy nature of the industry, colleagues are often placed in nearly round-the-clock proximity. The client cannot always provide permanent office space for the nomadic consultant, so it is not uncommon for a team to spend the entire day crammed into a small conference room. Colleagues may also share flights each week (the Airport Test in its truest form), breakfast in the hotel's frequent-guest "lounge" each morning, and dinner at a nearby restaurant each night. In consulting, more than in nearly all other professions, fitting in does not just make for a more enjoyable or tolerable workday; it is essential for survival.

"Well, it's nice to know that Elite3 values what really matters," I told Harrison, trying to pass off this sarcastic remark as genuine.

He bought it. "Exactly," he said, nodding enthusiastically. He smiled and locked eyes with me and held the gaze, like the high-five earlier, for just a second too long.

* * *

My time with Harrison did not end with a handshake or even a hug outside of the sports bar. I tried to initiate this sort of goodbye. Had I succeeded, I would not have had to call my boyfriend the next day to confess a story that resembled Quinn's memorable tale.

"Alex," I said solemnly as soon as he picked up the phone, "I did something last night that I shouldn't have done."

"Laura?" he responded, confused by a worrisome tone that rarely initiated our daily conversations and a groggy voice that was unbefitting of a 12:30 p.m. call. "I can't hear you very well. Can you speak up and repeat what you just said?"

"I—I did something last—" I stopped, unable to repeat it. "Yesterday afternoon I met Harrison, my buddy from Elite3, at Starbucks."

"I know," Alex said, "you had told me the other night that you'd be going."

"We met there to practice case interviews."

"I know. You told me that too."

"When we finished, Harrison invited me to a sports bar to watch the Duke game."

"OK," he responded hesitantly, as if conflicted between relief that a few drinks at a bar may have been all and fear that it was only the beginning. "Did you drink a lot?"

"No, not much."

"How much?"

"Just some beer."

"Beer?"

"Yeah," I admitted cautiously, wary of Alex's inevitable response.

"You *hate* beer!"

"I know," I said softly, acknowledging the truth I had been afraid of sharing with Harrison. "But I only had two."

"Did he try to get you to drink more than that?"

"He tried, but I said no," I proudly told Alex, eager to grab credit where I could. But as I boasted of my near sobriety, I found myself wishing I could've at least had a better excuse for my poor judgment.

"We left the bar," I continued, "and I told Harrison I'd walk home."

"But?" Alex countered, offering this transition because he knew, just as I had known, exactly what was coming next.

"But Harrison insisted that walking would be dangerous. So he flagged a cab for me."

"But?" he asked ominously, in confirmation of the predictability of Harrison's moves and another searing denunciation of my behavior.

"But then Harrison got inside the cab. I asked the driver to drop me off first, and Harrison told him otherwise."

"Of course he did." The words stung for their truth. That Harrison would try to pull something like this was not surprising; that I chose not to stop it *was*.

"The taxi arrived at his apartment. Harrison invited me up."

"Of course he did."

"I told him no. I said I wouldn't go up with him."

"And let me guess," Alex deadpanned, "he didn't listen."

I said nothing.

"Right?" Alex pressed.

Again, nothing. My silence was a tacit confirmation of Alex's suspicions.

"Laura, he ignored you—he ignored you, didn't he?"

I had nothing to say but knew I needed to say something. The longer the silence, the harder it would be to break it. I tried to share the story I had rehearsed in my head countless times before placing this call, but I could only think that Alex was right. Harrison *did* ignore me, and it was because I let him.

"Are you sure you don't want to come up?" he had asked kindly. He had leaned in and looked me in the eyes with a soft gaze, questioning my decision because he knew, just as Alex had implied, that if I truly meant no, I never would have found myself alone with him on a Saturday night in a cab outside of his apartment.

"Y-y-yeah," I stammered, breaking eye contact and looking down at my fidgeting hands. "Yes, I'm sure. I don't want to come up." As the words spilled out of my mouth and I tried placing meaning behind them, I knew that this was like my attempt at walking home or asking the driver to stop at my place first—a halfhearted defense that allowed me to pretend my rational side was still in control, though I knew it was not.

"Laura," Harrison spoke my name in a soft, caring voice that sent chills through my body, "I really think you should come up with me." He put his hand on my leg and held it there gently, then squeezed. "I really do." More chills.

With his hand resting halfway between my knee and my hip, he lifted his fingers, then let each one fall on my thigh, one at a time, before curling inward. He repeated this, again and again, and I could only think of the comment he'd made earlier at the bar: *You passed. You passed the Facebook test.* He had confessed this as I sat on a barstool, dumbstruck by this admission but also confused as to how I could have passed a screening for "fun" when my privacy settings concealed all photos except my play-it-safe, no-drink-in-hand profile picture. Apparently, Harrison had neglected to mention that, depending on the candidate's gender, the Facebook test assumes different forms. *Did you actually think it was a coincidence that we were assigned to be buddies?* he had asked. *I could tell from that one picture—you are hot.* It was a disgusting admission. And I, an insecure student in front of a consultant whose firm I aspired to join, was not unmoved by the flattery. Nor was I unaware of its implications. Though I may have earned my Elite3 interview based on my résumé, it was my appearance—not my qualifications—that had impressed, and would continue to impress, Harrison.

"So," he made another attempt, "what do you think? Will you join me?"

With each choice that Harrison presented to me, I was overtaken by the fear of upsetting the person I needed to impress, and with each *no* I delivered, I envisioned my chances at an Elite3 internship and—given my lack of options elsewhere—any summer internship slipping away. After a semester in New York rubbing elbows with, and in some cases being pursued by, the corporate and financial elite, I had difficulty accepting the harrowing possibility of returning to Alabama for the summer and working a minimum-wage job. It was just as distressing to think of my fellow internship-less classmates, many of whom would overcome the suffocating economy and find an impressive work experience with the help of their parents' network and pocketbook, and the surplus of employers eager for free labor. These peers' advantage in next fall's full-time job search, thanks to their bolstered résumés, could be insurmountable.

Hot. As I sat in the taxi, the words replayed in my mind—the way Harrison said *hot* slowly and in a breathy voice, enunciating the *t* with a sharpness that made me question any preconceived notions of right and wrong. I wondered if I had something, some sort of edge in this race, that my peers did not.

Harrison looked at me, but I could not maintain eye contact. I stared at the taxi's meter, which, in this stationary cab, was charging us for one thing—time. I watched it tick upward, a financial measure of my uncertainty.

"N-no. I can't come up with you," I managed to say. I shook my head for extra emphasis, a gesture that helped me feel some conviction in a decision made so hesitantly. "It wouldn't be right," I added, another attempt that was less about convincing Harrison of the validity of this reasoning and more about convincing myself.

This time, when Harrison heard *no*, he did not lean in with kind eyes and a warm smile. He did not place his hand on my leg and squeeze. A distraught look came over his face, alarming me with its jarring contrast to the persistent grin that, for the last few hours, had assured me that I was doing something right. The reaction was both chilling and familiar—it was the same display of disgust I had observed when Harrison suspected that I did not drink and when he disparaged the applicant with the boring Facebook profile. His judging eyes said it all: *You're not one of us.*

"That's not OK," he said harshly. "You're not being fair."

"What's not fair?"

"You cannot tell me," he shot back, "that you think it's acceptable to spend the whole evening together, take a cab back with me, and not accept my invitation to come up. You can't pretend like you didn't know what was going on."

"W-w-well, I thought we were just hanging out, you know?" I attempted. "I didn't think there was anything more to it. I didn't realize that—"

"Laura," he said my name again, but this time with a voice so stern and unforgiving that chills went through my body for a different reason. Harrison was about to snap. "Don't play dumb."

I felt as if I had been slapped across the face. I had a difficult time believing that following Harrison to his apartment could help, rather than harm, my chances with Elite3, but so much about this recruiting process had already made no sense. Reason was obsolete and the paradoxes astounding. There was Quinn, whose dalliance on a gay chat site led to internship gold his sophomore summer and—as he learned just days after recounting that appalling story to Paris and me—an offer with a major i-bank for his junior summer. There was Paris, who, as far as I knew at the time, had not committed any such salacious acts but was nevertheless a bombshell who embraced her sex appeal and found unparalleled success. These two were the only ones in the Duke–in–New York program with offers. Maybe they were on to something.

"I—I—" I tried to speak, but no words came out.

After successfully delivering consecutive nos, however unconvincing they were, I lost all momentum. In the panic incited by Harrison's accusation, I revealed just how desperate I was to keep him happy.

"B-b-but—" I tried. Again, nothing.

Feeling empowered, Harrison broke the silence with a bold statement that—given his propensity to speak the unspeakable all night—should not have surprised me. But it did.

"Paris did it."

"Excuse me?"

"Paris came up."

I stared blankly.

"Paris is your roommate, right?"

"W-w-well, yes. Yes, she is. But how do you know her?"

"She's also interviewing with Elite3. I'm her buddy, too."

"Oh." My heart sank. I should have known. Although Paris had insisted that she would accept the J.P. Morgan offer if it arrived, when it did, she had a change of heart. *I simply don't know what to do!* she would bemoan to her phone coterie. *All these banking offers are just fantastic, but now I'm becoming especially interested in the consulting industry.* With so many offers yet to be claimed, she could not possibly throw in the towel. Employers were the stingiest they had perhaps ever been, and she was grabbing up one after another of a commodity in short supply. Offers were Paris's drug, and she could not get enough.

"On Thursday, Paris and—" Harrison began, but he did not need to say anything more. I found myself nodding as I recalled what happened a few nights earlier when I had awoken to Paris stumbling into our room and smelling of alcohol long after she had skipped out the door with what now seemed to be the famous last words of Harrison's targets: *I'm just running out to meet someone for coffee and practice case interviews.*

"She," Harrison said firmly, "came back with me."

He cocked his head to the side and stared at me with a smirk, confident in the effectiveness of a claim so slimy and appalling, but also brilliant. He rightly assumed that I possessed the singular quality that defines so many aspiring bankers and consultants—an unbounded and unabashed competitiveness that is less about being your best and more about besting others. I did not know if Harrison was telling the truth, but by revealing Paris's apparent tactic for getting ahead, he expected me to one-up her. And I was tempted.

Harrison had successfully provoked that same damned instinct that had sucked me into this frenzied job hunt, so eager for the thrill of pursuing the most challenging and prestigious path, no matter the personal cost.

"Look, Laura," he told me, "I know you have a boyfriend, but Paris does, too. She didn't let that stop her."

That Paris succumbed should not have surprised me any more than Harrison's expectation that I would do the same. Paris belonged at an elite consultancy like Harrison's firm or an elite investment bank like the ones clamoring to make her one of their own. She belonged at those places because they were just like her—flawless, seductive exteriors that belied a less glamorous truth.

"C'mon, Laura." Harrison unbuckled his seat belt and reached for his wallet to pay the taxi fare, whose total derived more from waiting time than driving time.

He started to open the door. "C'mon, Laura, I know you want to."

* * *

"Alex, I'm sorry," I told my boyfriend, who had sat on the line, silent, as I related the entire story.

When I finished, he did not yell or curse or retaliate. He thanked me for being honest and calling to confess.

"I'm sorry," I said again, and I was. "I feel awful. I feel terrible." And I did—emotionally *and* physically. I had awakened that morning with my head spinning, an urge to throw up, and regret for allowing things to get out of hand the night before. I felt hungover even though—despite Harrison's best efforts—I had not been drunk. At least, not on alcohol.

My decision to go up with Harrison was not unlike the decisions I had made since submitting myself to the internship chase—I lost control of my own behavior. With Harrison, as with the recruiting process, the speed was dizzying and the peer pressure overpowering.

"Laura, how did you let this happen? What made you think that going up with him was a good idea?" Alex asked calmly, his voice barely above a whisper. He was more hurt than angry.

I did not know how to explain that I had become so swept up in the recruiting madness that I did not recognize the person making my choices, or that I was so far removed from my comfort zone that it seemed easier to run with it than correct my path.

"I don't know. I don't know how this happened."

I defended my behavior with trite excuses. *But nothing actually happened*, I told Alex, even though he and I both knew that, in too many ways, so much had. *But I didn't sleep with him. I didn't even kiss him*, I said, as if I somehow deserved praise for, finally, doing what I knew was right.

It was when Harrison had led me into his room, sat on his bed, and patted the mattress beside him for me to join him that I did what I should have done much earlier in the evening. I fled.

"Laura," Alex pressed, "please answer my question. You can't just say 'I don't know.' Why did you let this happen? Why'd you ever let it get that far?"

The question was fair, and all too familiar. I had been asked *Why?* countless times in the past two months. *Why Duke? Why economics? Why this bank? Why this consulting firm?* and—most famously—*Why finance?* and *Why consulting?* In interview after interview, I had answered these questions skillfully, spinning lies without a thought of the truth I was avoiding.

"Laura, just tell me what you were thinking."

This time, and for the first time, I could not lie. Finally, someone was holding me accountable.

"That's the thing, Alex. I wasn't thinking. I haven't been thinking." I paused and took a deep breath, at first surprised by the words coming out of my mouth and then surprised by how right they sounded: "I have no idea why I'm doing this."

YEAR 3, SEMESTER 2, THROUGH YEAR 4, SEMESTER 2

Think of all the profits produced by businesses operating in the U.S. as a cake. Twenty-five years ago, the slice taken by financial firms was about a seventh of the whole. Last year, it was more than a quarter. (In 2006, at the peak of the boom, it was about a third.) In other words, during a period in which American companies have created iPhones, Home Depot, and Lipitor, the best place to work has been in an industry that doesn't design, build, or sell a single tangible thing.

—John Cassidy, "What Good Is Wall Street?"
The New Yorker, November 29, 2010

CHAPTER 10

No

As of March 1—that dreaded date and omen of an insignificant summer—I had no offers. I initiated Plan B, scouring the Internet and Duke's career resources for paid internships. I applied to any position that solicited applications and found ways to submit a résumé to many that didn't.

On March 6, I interviewed with a small consulting firm. Two days later, my interviewer e-mailed me with news that budget cuts were forcing the firm to cut its internship program.

On March 9, I turned 21. That same day, the Dow closed at a 12-year low.

On April 1, I called my parents and asked whether they would financially support me over the summer if I had to adopt Plan C and apply to unpaid positions. I do not know if it was more difficult for me to ask this of my parents or for them to have to tell me no.

And then, on April 10, the first offer arrived. One week later, the second one did. And one day after that, the third.

The first offer came from a large insurance company and resulted from my cold-calling efforts: "Hello, my name is Laura Newland. I'm a junior at Duke University, and I was wondering if there are any internships for . . ." After hearing my pitch, the company had asked for my résumé, scheduled a phone interview, held a follow-up, and then extended an offer. It all unfolded in under three weeks—an unfamiliar, wondrously functional process.

The second offer was on its way, I was assured, but I withdrew before it officially arrived. This one came from a consulting firm that recruited on campus and bungled the process: the monthlong silence following the submission of my application; the last-minute, expenses-paid flight to Washington, D.C., and hotel stay for a single 30-minute case-study interview, a tour of an office largely vacated by the recently laid-off employees, and meet-and-greets with executives who uncomfortably dodged questions about the news-making cuts; and the promises to call, following this overnight visit, that came and went, again and again, as budget problems were blamed. Then, finally, I was told an offer would come. I withdrew before it did.

And then there was the golden offer, which arrived in the fashion I had envisioned since that early week in New York when I attended the J.P. Morgan interview with Paris, and her phone rang days later and mine did not. This time, it was my phone ringing and displaying the 212 area code during the one-week window.

"Hi Laura," the recruiter, a woman named Melanie, said. Her voice was friendly and enthusiastic, and this could mean only one thing. "After meeting with you over the last few weeks, we are so excited for you to join us this summer."

There it was. The Offer. Even though it came at the semester's bitter end, this was not an internship I would be settling for—this was the opportunity I had dreamed of. Melanie was inviting me to spend the summer at a private equity firm.

"Thank you, Melanie. That's—"

"We ask," she interrupted, "that you start your internship the first week of June and that you stay with us until— "

"Excuse me—" I tried again, but Melanie was on a roll, so eager to rattle off details about the offer and the summer and the firm.

My relationship with this employer had begun early in the semester when I attended an interview in February. I did not hear a word until April, when Melanie reached out and explained that, contrary to my assumption, I had impressed the interviewer two months prior. The firm had liked me all along. Budget issues had forced termination of the internship program, and now it was being reinstated. Would I like to return for another interview? she wanted to know.

And so began a series of visits to the small, all-male office, where I interviewed, one-on-one, with each of the 15 men. Many of them spoke fondly of their previous intern, named Jessica, and with their offer to me they were poised to bring a young woman into the frat house for the summer again.

"I'm e-mailing you the paperwork as we speak," Melanie continued, "so if you could please print it, sign it, and send it back to me, we can make the whole thing official. How does that sound?"

Had the offer arrived in February, following the initial interview with the firm, I would have thought this sounded wonderful, convinced not only that the internship would make me the envy of countless peers but also that it was—especially in these economic times—the opportunity of a lifetime. Because then, Harrison had not yet exposed the ways in which the recruiting process was distorting my perceptions. Paris and Quinn had not yet established themselves as the only ones in our program to receive offers from Wall Street, surely a reflection of the culture awaiting there. And I had not yet attended many of our program's exclusive visits to banks, where I witnessed a behind-the-scenes reality so unlike the rosy image I had fallen for on campus. When the office tours, lunches, and recruiting presentations were part of just another day at the office—instead of an expenses-paid jaunt to campus—the young bankers did not exude any of their trademark pep and passion. There was little gushing and much complaining—about the hours, the pressure, the culture, the banality of what they did.

"I'm so sorry to interrupt," I finally interjected, successfully. "I want to thank you for calling and thank the firm for extending this offer, but"—I paused, as surprised by how easily these words left my mouth as Melanie would be by what they were—"I'm not going to be accepting it."

Silence.

"Excuse me?" Her eloquent, professional tone turned terse.

"I appreciate this opportunity, and I've appreciated—"

"What?" she snapped, increasingly agitated, as though she was gradually comprehending what was happening.

"I—"

"What?" Now her voice boomed into the phone, the progression complete. "You're not taking our offer?"

"Yes, that's right."

"But do you realize"—she was panicky, and though I had expected confusion and disappointment, this reaction was full of anger—"that you're the only candidate we sent to our final round?"

"No, I didn't realize—"

"If you don't take this, we won't have an intern for the summer!"

I wondered if Melanie and my interviewers had considered the possibility that someone would turn down this type of opportunity in this economy. "I'm sorry to hear that."

"Well, can you at least tell me why you won't be accepting?"

There was no point in explaining that as I had met with each of the firm's employees, I was unable to envision myself working there and actually enjoying it. And that was when I realized something that no one had told me about recruiting: interviews were as much an opportunity for *me* to judge the employers as they were for the employers to judge me. Just as interviewers pass over candidates for being, as the rejection letters often say, "not the right fit," I too had the power, and the responsibility, to reject an employer for being a poor match. What seemed a radical concept at first only made more sense the more I thought about it.

"I'll be accepting a different opportunity," I told Melanie.

"I see. Well, then, where on Wall Street will you be going instead?"

"I'm actually not going to be working on Wall Street."

"Oh?"

"I've also been interviewing with an insurance company and—"

That's when she lost it. "Insurance?" she cried into the phone. Melanie was just a recruiter, but she understood that in her world of finance there was an indisputable hierarchy. Private equity was at or near the top. Insurance was somewhere far beneath it.

"Insurance? You're turning down a Wall Street job to work in insurance?"

No, this was not what I was doing, but I did not feel the need to explain that instead of forsaking Wall Street for some insurance company, I was simply forsaking Wall Street. I was, to put it bluntly, over it. And contrary to Melanie's assumption, I was not turning down one finance role simply to take another, less "prestigious" one. That is because the insurance company had offered me an internship that had nothing to do with insurance. I had been given an opportunity to work at the headquarters of a large company and help with a project that sounded innovative, valuable, and, well, *interesting*.

"Yes, I'll be interning with an insurance company." I paused, giving her the opportunity to gasp again. This time, I heard a sigh instead.

"They are," I continued, "hoping to make all of their offices across the country more energy efficient. They're looking into environmentally friendly alternatives and need some help from an intern as they launch their companywide green initiative."

She was unsure of how to respond, so I filled the silence. "I'm very excited to learn more about this field. It's incredibly relevant today."

"I see," she deadpanned.

The day before my call with Melanie, I had talked with the man who would be my supervisor for the internship I was accepting, and he spoke in detail about the opportunities I would have over the summer: traveling across the country to study the many offices' energy consumption, learning about new environmentally friendly technologies, exploring ways to get employees on board for the organizationwide change.

"I hope," I told Melanie, "you understand that—"

"I see," she said again, "I see."

The call ended quickly. I left to run some errands and, for the first time in months, did not carry my phone with me. I returned to a voicemail from the private equity firm's managing director: "Laura, I was so sorry to hear that you are considering accepting a different offer. All of us here were so impressed with you, and I want to assure you that this offer is still yours, should you want it. Please, Laura, give me a call back so we can talk. It's not too late to change your mind."

I considered it disrespectful to ignore his message, so I called him back. But I did not change my mind.

I had thought that saying no to the managing director, over his warnings of the serious mistake I was sure to regret, would be vindicating. But it was defeating. I was pleased to dismiss the internship and, with it, the near guarantee of securing a position after graduation with that or many other Wall Street firms. I was excited for my summer opportunity that awaited, but as satisfying as it was to close the door on Wall Street, it was disheartening and shameful to realize that during my time in college, I had failed to open many others.

* * *

The internship I accepted that summer did not open new and different doors, either, as I had hoped it would. Despite all that was described and promised while recruiting me, the company's nationwide "green initiative" proved to be less of an initiative and more of an opportunity for one overworked property manager to let an overeager college student take over his neglected duty of collecting electric and water bills from the offices across the country—no travel included—and crunching some numbers.

The disappointment I felt was powerful but, contrary to the grave warning of the private equity firm's managing director, not powerful enough to make me regret turning down his firm's internship. That is because my confidence in knowing I was not meant for Wall Street, despite all I had invested to get there, was unwavering. Unfortunately, my certainty of what I did *not* want was as strong as my uncertainty of what I did.

So I would find a job, I decided. If I could, of course, given the crippled economy that showed few signs of recovery. Employment seemed my only option, as there was no justification for acquiring additional debt to "figure it all out" as a graduate student when I had failed to do so as an undergraduate.

I was not alone in this. Like many students, I had found comfort in the depiction of college as a bastion of academic inquiry and self-discovery. Duke did much to deliver on this expectation; it would be dishonest to imply otherwise and disrespectful to the many remarkable professors, peers, and opportunities I discovered there. And yet as graduation neared, and with it the inevitable reflection on a memorable and expensive four years, I could not help but feel that there was a part of my college experience that I had been wholly unprepared for. The career opportunities available to a school's students and the career paths of its graduates are too often unmentioned to prospective students, perhaps because of the unflattering reality on many campuses: the pre-professionalism so pervasive that freshmen must scramble to find—and pay for—internships; the employers that begin targeting sophomores with recruiting campaigns so elaborate that many a student is persuaded to leave her do-gooding nature at the door; and the debt at both the undergraduate and graduate levels that distorts students' priorities. For me, an unawareness of all these things precipitated my slow, difficult adjustment and the perception of falling so dangerously behind that as I struggled to get back on track, I allowed the voices of others to silence my own.

These less glamorous slices of college life are easily obscured because the success of universities and the multibillion-dollar college-prep industry depends largely on promoting the romanticized image of college that prospective students and their parents *want* to believe. If a marketing effort promises anything less, fewer students will apply to that school (thus lowering its ranking), and fewer parents will pony up for that book or service that promises to boost one's chances of "getting in." The result is a misguided dialogue about today's college experience.

Maybe this is why I spent too much of college feeling lost and why, by the end of it, I felt transformed and grateful—and yet I had lost much of that strong sense of empowerment with which I had arrived. I would, along with many of my peers, take a guess about what I was meant to do after graduation, hoping to get lucky and stumble upon it on the first go. Some of us would figure it out down the road and others never at all. I could only hope that one day I would.

It was my feeling of disempowerment that left me thinking often about the culture on college campuses and the forces that are influencing the next generation of leaders. Recognizing the need for more-honest conversation about today's college experience made me realize how I could feel empowered by my own. I would share it.

Epilogue

MY STORY DOES not have the vindicating ending in which I forgo the well-paying corporate job to take a chance at the career of my dreams. I am still working to reach that part. On some days I feel closer than on others as I attempt a balance between the two ends of that spectrum: my days spent at the corporate job, my weekends and the wee hours of the morning dedicated to doing what I love. It is an incongruous coupling, and it may not be that concise, feel-good conclusion to my recruiting journey, but for my story and especially for these times, it is a realistic one. And for me, for now, it works.

One side of this balance came about during my senior year, when I unconditionally crossed Wall Street off my career list and worked tirelessly with the Career Center to find unique alternatives—to a maddening, unsuccessful end. Ultimately I accepted an offer from a consulting firm.

The opposing side of the balance transpired soon after I accepted this job. Recognizing my failure in college to discover what I loved, I resolved to do with the next years of my life what had eluded me the previous four. It was during my last semester, removed from the rat race on campus and the up-or-out environment awaiting at work, that I started writing. This new hobby could not be attributed to any English class I took at Duke (I avoided these), any professor who praised and encouraged my writing skills (none had), or any long-held interest of mine. Instead, one day I felt compelled to share my story, and I began to write it. Writing was unplanned and unfamiliar and did not come easily to me. Unlike nearly everything that had consumed me before, my new hobby offered no one to compete against or impress. If success was defined as telling a story that people wanted to read, my chance of success was low. And yet I found a love for writing, enjoying it so much that I questioned how the work awaiting at my new job could possibly provide as much happiness.

Feeling inspired by an undertaking that wondrously occupied nearly every free hour of those last college months, I requested a late start date from my employer. After graduating and before making my northbound journey to start work, I took a southbound detour, moving in with my parents for what would be one of Alabama's hottest summers on record. It was the best summer I ever had because I spent it writing and learning how it felt to love what I did.

Summer ended, and by the time that work began, I had gained an entirely different perspective on what I did, and did not, want out of it. The opportunity to pay down my loans and acquire valuable experience—while figuring out what was next and finishing a half-complete manuscript—was important. A taxing career, in which I was driven by what my peers wanted and what my superiors wanted for me, was not.

Identifying my priorities has given me that feeling of control I lacked in college. Because I have discovered what my passion is, I have not allowed myself to grow consumed by what my passion is not.

For now, I enjoy my job and love writing, and I hope that, sometime soon, the latter will help to create new and different career opportunities. I look back fondly on my college experience, but I wish that I had been better prepared. I share my story with hopes that the dialogue about higher education can begin to evolve into a wider discussion about universities' responsibility in shaping a generation. Whether these schools are fulfilling the needs of society—and also meeting the obligations that come with tens and sometimes hundreds of thousands in cost—is not questioned enough. It is only after altering the way that colleges are represented and discussed that we can begin changing the culture. This is of course a daunting task, as shown by the many forces that, for me, contributed to a college experience in which Wall Street played an oversized role: it is as easy to blame the deep-pocketed recruiters as the colleges that open their doors to them without offering sufficient alternatives; it is as much the fault of a higher-education industry that leaves undergraduate and graduate students with crushing debt as of a job market that values financial engineers more than actual engineers; and it is as attributable to the parents who have raised an entitled and overscheduled generation as to the students like me who lose sight of themselves and avoid taking risks because we are so afraid of failing.

The consequences vary by school and will shift over time, but as long as the student debt load keeps climbing—in 2012, it topped $1 trillion—and tuition costs continue to outpace inflation, the brain drain from more productive careers will continue to highlight one of society's ills: we charge heftily for an education and then foolishly expect the educated to use their diplomas for the benefit of society.

Acknowledgments

THIS BOOK IS dedicated to my mom and dad, whose appearance on just a few pages cannot convey the commitment of two parents who always put their daughters' interests before their own. Every page, however, is imprinted with the influence of these tireless reviewers and advisers, who empowered me with their confidence because that is what they have always done, and it is what they do best.

I am grateful for the humbling displays of support by the others who embraced this project as if it were their own: my sister, Erica, whose judgment I trust more than anyone else's and rely on often; Sarah Jenkins, who was an endless source of advice, laughs, and perspective; and Amber Heinrich, whose savvy and creativity were indispensable at many turning points.

Some brave souls read early versions of the manuscript and offered encouragement and advice: David Tat; Kevin Lieberman; Audrey Cardell; Scott Jenkins; Enoch and Amy Lipson; and my wonderful uncle and aunt, Martin and Stephanie Jackel, whose support means so much. The wisdom of other friends and mentors has left its mark on this book, so I owe a big thank-you to Alida Al-Saadi, Claire Lukens, Ryan Genkin, Jackie Sink, Josh Sommer, Dan Certner, George Grody, and Stephen Jackel.

I am appreciative of the many people who agreed to share their experiences and perspectives to supplement my own. While researching the dynamics of campus recruiting, I was impressed by the openness of Duke's Career Center and the commitment of Executive Director William Wright-Swadel (whose first year at Duke was my last) to address many of the issues I wrote about. It was wonderful to work with Elissa Rabellino, who provided thorough copyediting and expert guidance. The professionalism of Dennis Gallagher, Mark Rhynsburger, and Paul Rapp also helped carry this project to the finish line.

And, finally, a most heartfelt thank-you to someone who entered my life after much of this book was written yet still found a way to influence it in the greatest ways. I owe so much to Cory, for everything, but especially for pushing me to give this book my best, even when it brought out my worst, and for always believing, even when I did not, that I had this in me.

Notes

Prologue

more graduates took jobs on Wall Street than anywhere else—"Class of 2008 Statistics," Duke University Student Affairs, http://studentaffairs.duke.edu/career/statistics-reports/career-center-senior-survey/class-2008-statistics.

finance was the most popular industry for graduates of Harvard, Columbia, Duke, Georgetown, and even the University of Pennsylvania's engineering school—"Harvard College Seniors 2012: Next Steps," Harvard Office of Career Services, http://www.ocs.fas.harvard.edu/next_steps.htm; "Career Center Senior Survey Class of 2012," Duke University Student Affairs, http://studentaffairs.duke.edu/career/statistics-reports/career-center-senior-survey; "University of Pennsylvania School of Engineering and Applied Science Undergraduate Career Plans Survey Report 2011–2012," University of Pennsylvania Career Services, http://www.vpul.upenn.edu/careerservices/files/SEAS_2012cp.pdf (my source for the statistic that the finance industry attracted the most graduates can be found in the "All Employed Respondents by Industry" graph); "2012 Graduating Student Survey Results: Columbia College (CC) and the Fu Foundation School of Engineering and Applied Science," Columbia University Center for Career Education, http://www.careereducation.columbia.edu/sites/cce/files/2012_gss--cc__seas-ug.pdf; "Class of 2012 Senior Survey," Georgetown University, http://careercenter.georgetown.edu/document/1242785463822/class-of-2012-senior-survey-book.pdf.

the number of graduates heading into finance was nearly three times higher than the number entering medical school—"Annual Report 2011–2012," Career Services at Princeton University, http://www.princeton.edu/career/pdfs/Princeton-Career-Services-2011-2012-Annual-Report.pdf. My source for the statistic that Princeton graduates were nearly three times more likely to accept a finance job than enter medical school can be found on pages 7 (40 students enrolling in medical school) and 12 (97 students accepted jobs as analyst [investment banking] and 15 accepted jobs in sales/trading [finance]).

Chapter 1

American colleges and universities seem to be in every business but education — Jeffrey Selingo, *College Unbound: The Future of Higher Education and What It Means for Students* (New York: New Harvest, 2013).

tied with Stanford and placed higher than half of the Ivy League — Sarah Ball, "U.S. News drops Duke to 8th place," *Chronicle*, Duke University, August 24, 2006, http://www.dukechronicle.com/articles/2006/08/25/us-news-drops-duke-8th-place.

Chapter 2

for others better suited to meet repayment schedules — Andrew Hacker and Claudia Dreifus, "The Debt Crisis at American Colleges," *Atlantic*, August 17, 2011.

Chapter 3

some people are asking whether it's worth it for the graduates and for the country — "Is a Job on Wall Street Still Worth It?" Narrated by Jeremy Hobson, American Public Media's *Marketplace*, May 25, 2010, http://www.marketplace.org/topics/business/job-wall-street-still-worth-it.

for those accepted to the exclusive overnight events — J.P. Morgan and Morgan Stanley are two of the banks that host paid internship programs specifically for sophomores and even freshmen, while Goldman Sachs and Credit Suisse are two of the banks that offer one- or two-day-long educational and networking programs at their offices. More about these programs can be found at https://www.credit-suisse.com/careers/campus_recruiting/en/americas/internship_programs.jsp, http://www.goldmansachs.com/careers/why-goldman-sachs/diversity/diversity-us.html, http://careers.jpmorgan.com/student/jpmorgan/careers/us/programs/summerug/intern, and http://www.morganstanley.com/about/careers/ischolarships_na.html.

Chapter 4

worried more about carving out a tangible path for their futures — Elizabeth S. Auritt and Delphine Rodrik, "The Fall of Academics at Harvard," *Harvard Crimson*, February 28, 2013.

these five banks alone had paid their employees $39 billion in bonuses — Christine Harper, "Wall Street Bonuses Hit Record $39 Billion for 2007 (Update3)," January 17, 2008, http://www.bloomberg.com/apps/ news?pid=newsarchive&sid=aPXU4y.z8E9o&refer=us.

taking on the average $167,000 debt load of a medical student — "October 2012 Medical Student Education: Debt, Costs, and Loan Repayment Fact Card," Association of American Medical Colleges, https://www. aamc.org/download/152968/data.

undergraduate debt, which in 2012 averaged about $27,000 — Tamar Lewin, "Student-Loan Borrowers Average $26,500 in Debt," *New York Times,* http://www.nytimes.com/2012/10/18/education/report-says-average-student-loan-debt-is-up-to-26500.html.

more than 10 times the salary of an equally experienced cancer researcher or aerospace engineer — "Traders' Smaller Bonuses Still Top Pay for Brain Surgeons, 4-Star Generals," *Bloomberg,* January 13, 2011, http://www .bloomberg.com/news/2011-01-13/traders-smaller-bonuses-still-top-pay-for-brain-surgeons-4-star-generals.html.

hailed from 46 states and 41 countries — "The Class of 2010 by the Numbers," *Duke Today,* September 6, 2006, http://today.duke.edu/2006/09/ class2010.html.

volleyball on the beach is an unnecessary pit stop for anyone who intends to win it — Shining Li, "The death of summer," *Chronicle,* Duke University, June 30, 2010, http://www.dukechronicle.com/articles/2010/07/01/ death-summer.

buying internships outright in online charity auctions — Sue Shellenbarger, "Do You Want an Internship? It'll Cost You," *Wall Street Journal,* January 28, 2009, http://online.wsj.com/article/NA_WSJ_ PUB:SB123310699999022549.html.

can reach $11,000 for eight weeks — "IB Immersion + Internship Placement Program Tuition," Dream Careers Global Internship Programs, http://summerinternships.com/newyork/ibanking/tuition/.

double what it was when I was born—U.S. Department of Education, National Center for Education Statistics. *Digest of Education Statistics, 2011* (NCES 2012-001), Chapter 3, http://nces.ed.gov/programs/digest/d11/ch_3.asp.

can earn over $30,000 in just one summer—Kevin Roose, "Fewer Perks and More Work for Wall St.'s Summer Interns," Dealbook, *New York Times*, July 21, 2011, http://dealbook.nytimes.com/2011/07/21/fewer-perks-and-more-work-for-wall-st-s-summer-interns/.

stock price spent the month fluctuating between $75 and $90—Daniel Burns, "12 key dates in the demise of Bear Stearns," Reuters, March 17, 2008, http://blogs.reuters.com/from-reuterscom/2008/03/17/12-key-dates-in-the-demise-of-bear-stearns/.

J.P. Morgan purchased Bear Stearns for the fire-sale price of $2 a share—Andrew Ross Sorkin, "JP Morgan Pays $2 a Share for Bear Stearns," *New York Times*, March 17, 2008, http://www.nytimes.com/2008/03/17/business/17bear.html?pagewanted=all.

they lived off the bankrupt firm's $10,000 signing bonus—Louise Story, "Bear Stearns's New Hires Become Job Seekers," *New York Times*, April 19, 2008, http://www.nytimes.com/2008/04/19/business/19bear.html?pagewanted=1&_r=1&sq=bear%20stearns%20senior%20job%20offers&st=cse&scp=1.

finance was still the most popular industry—"Class of 2009 Statistics," Duke University Student Affairs, http://studentaffairs.duke.edu/career/statistics-reports/career-center-senior-survey/class-2009-statistics; "Next Steps for Harvard Seniors: 2011," Office of Career Services, Harvard University, http://www.ocs.fas.harvard.edu/students/jobs/seniorsurvey.htm (my source for the statistic that more Harvard graduates in 2009 accepted jobs in finance than any other industry can be found in the "College Trend" figure that compares graduates' career paths from 2006 to 2011); "Career Plans Survey College of Arts and Sciences—Class of 2009," University of Pennsylvania Career Services, http://www.vpul.upenn.edu/careerservices/files/Class2009CareerPlans_1344547763.pdf.

Tuesday's Career and Summer Opportunities Fair—Cate Harding, "Students scramble to schmooze at Career Fair," *Chronicle*, Duke University, January 15, 2008, http://www.dukechronicle.com/articles/2008/01/16/students-scramble-schmooze-career-fair.

attracted applications from 18 percent of Harvard's class of 2010—James Lu, "TFA no. 1 for Yalies," *Yale Daily News*, October 13, 2010, http://yaledailynews.com/blog/2010/10/13/tfa-no-1-for-yalies/.

the top employer of graduates of Yale, Duke, and Georgetown—Michael Winerip, "A Chosen Few Are Teaching for America," *New York Times*, July 11, 2010, http://www.nytimes.com/2010/07/12/education/12winerip.html?_r=1&hp.

Are you going to admit defeat?—Interview with a Duke University graduate, February 2010. Name withheld by mutual agreement.

Chapter 5

our system incentivizes high-stakes gambling . . . rather than the rebooting and rebuilding of America—Frank Rich, "Who Killed the Disneyland Dream?" *New York Times*, December 25, 2010, http://www.nytimes.com/2010/12/26/opinion/26rich.html?pagewanted=all.

the sixth-highest tally on record—Ben White, "What Red Ink? Wall Street Paid Hefty Bonuses," *New York Times*, January 28, 2009, http://www.nytimes.com/2009/01/29/business/29bonus.html.

sophomores are now the intended audience—"Duke in NY: Financial Markets and Institutions," Duke University Economics, http://econ.duke.edu/DukeinNY.

a six-week experience during the summer, in London—"Duke in London: Finance," Duke University Economics, http://econ.duke.edu/undergraduate/study-away/duke-in-london.

Chapter 6

never intended to work in finance but don't have any better ideas about where to go — Ezra Klein, "Harvard's Liberal-Arts Failure Is Wall Street's Gain," *Bloomberg*, December 15, 2012, http://www.bloomberg.com/news/2012-02-16/harvard-liberal-arts-failure-is-wall-street-gain-commentary-by-ezra-klein.html.

interviews in finance often test an applicant's tolerance for such an environment — D. Bhatawedekhar, Dan Jacobson, Hussam Hamadeh, William Jarvis, and the staff of Vault, *Vault Guide to Finance Interviews* (New York: Vault.com Inc., 2008).

Over 250 people apply for just one position — Interview with an employee of the Duke Career Center, August 12, 2010. Name withheld by mutual agreement.

the real experience of a Duke student named Charlie — Interview with a Duke University student, August 10, 2010. Name changed by mutual agreement.

stranded in an airport for eight hours with this person — Bhatawedekhar et al., *Vault Guide to Finance Interviews.*

Chapter 7

banks like people in debt who will kill themselves for the big bonus — Bhatawedekhar et al., *Vault Guide to Finance Interviews.*

fetching coffee and ordering lunch — Gabriel Kim, Sarah Rodbard, and the Staff of Vault, *Vault Career Guide to Sales and Trading* (New York: Vault.com Inc., 2007).

the U.S. economy had shed 2.6 million jobs in the previous year alone — Louis Uchitelle, "U.S. lost 2.6 million jobs in 2008," *New York Times*, January 9, 2009, http://www.nytimes.com/2009/01/09/business/worldbusiness/09iht-jobs.4.19232394.html.

for doing nothing more than minimum-wage-type work — "Wage and Hour Law," New York State Department of Labor, http://www.labor.state.ny.us/workerprotection/laborstandards/workprot/lshmpg.shtm.

to be well liked, or at least not piss anyone off—Kim et al., *Vault Career Guide to Sales and Trading.*

Chapter 8

away from medicine and into, say, investment banking—Karen Sibert, "Don't Quit This Day Job," *New York Times,* June 11, 2011, http://www.nytimes.com/2011/06/12/opinion/12sibert.html?pagewanted=all.

Chapter 9

it was the money and the fact everyone else was doing it—Roger Cohen, "The King Is Dead," *New York Times,* September 17, 2008, http://www.nytimes.com/2008/09/18/opinion/18cohen.html.

doesn't stop until you get a case question—Marc P. Cosentino, *Case in Point: Complete Case Interview Preparation,* 5th ed. (Needham, MA: Burgee Press, 2007).

Chapter 10

an industry that doesn't design, build, or sell a single tangible thing—John Cassidy, "What Good Is Wall Street?" *New Yorker,* November 29, 2010.

the Dow closed at a 12-year low—Betsy Stark, "Tracking the Dow One Year After Rock Bottom," ABC News, March 9, 2010, http://abcnews.go.com/Business/year-ago-today-dow-hit-bottom-recession/story?id=10046578#.UXLKs8p3dM8.

Epilogue

the student debt load keeps climbing—in 2012, it topped $1 trillion—Josh Mitchell and Maya Jackson-Randall, "Student-Loan Debt Tops $1 Trillion," *Wall Street Journal,* March 22, 2012, http://online.wsj.com/article/SB10001424052702303381290457729593004760484846.html.

About Laura Newland

Laura Newland grew up in Auburn, Alabama, a small college town with an 87,000-seat football stadium and just one high school. She attended Duke University and began writing *Chasing Zeroes* during her final semester. In 2010, Newland graduated cum laude with a bachelor of science in economics. She moved to Philadelphia for a new job and finished *Chasing Zeroes* by writing for hours every morning before heading to the office. Newland now lives, works, and writes in Chicago. Her work has appeared in the *New York Times DealBook* and the *Huffington Post*. Learn more and get in touch at LauraNewland.com.

Made in the USA
Coppell, TX
22 February 2023

13266046R00129